HOW TO START A
HOME-BASED
PHOTOGRAPHY
BUSINESS

2nd edition

by Kenn Oberrecht

The Globe Pequot Press

OLD SAYBROOK, CONNECTICUT

FOR MY OLD FRIEND CHUCK KEIM

Cover and text design by Nancy Freeborn

Library of Congress Cataloging-in-Publication Data

Oberrecht, Kenn
   How to start a home-based photography business / Kenn Oberrecht—2nd ed.
       p.   cm.— (How to start a home-based business series)
   Includes index.
   ISBN 1-56440-986-4
   1. Photography—Business methods.   2. Home-based businesses.
   I. Title. II. Series.
   TR581.024 1996
   770'.68—dc20   96-12838
                                                                         CIP

Manufactured in the United States of America
Second Edition/First Printing

CONTENTS

5 THE LEGAL ASPECTS OF YOUR PHOTOGRAPHY BUSINESS / 73

6 WRITING A BUSINESS PLAN / 93

7 TAXES AND RECORD KEEPING / 109

INTRODUCTION

People working out of their homes now represent America's fastest-growing segment of the labor force. And why shouldn't they? Long commutes in bumper-to-bumper traffic are boring, expensive, time-consuming, nerve-wracking, and getting worse every day; mass transit isn't much better.

Meanwhile, technological advances have made working at home far easier and more irresistible than ever. Personal computers have become superfast and powerful. Software programs are advancing so rapidly the hardware manufacturers can't keep up. Fax machines, modems, fiber optics, and satellite links have made global communications practically flawless and nearly instantaneous. And all this functions as readily from a house, condominium, apartment, or mobile home as it does from a complex of corporate offices.

Among the many businesses people can operate out of their homes, photography ranks with the most suitable. Impact on the neighborhood ranges from minimal to nonexistent, start-up costs are relatively low, and it's possible to gradually phase into the business with little financial risk.

So this is a book for photographers—but it's not about photography. Rather, it covers the *business* of photography and tells you what you need to know about operating such a business from your home. In the chapters that follow, you'll find plenty of solid, practical information and many tips and tricks that will help you tap your photographic skills to earn a living.

CHAPTER ONE

GETTING STARTED AS A HOME-BASED PHOTOGRAPHER

Photography is not a profession that someone just happens on or stumbles into. Most of us become photographers for the same reason some people become kayakers or whale watchers—because we like it. The big difference is that it's hard to make a living paddling a kayak or waiting for whales to show up, whereas competent professional photographers are always in demand.

Most of us, nevertheless, begin as hobbyists. Some remain casual shutterbugs, content with taking occasional snapshots of friends and family or the dreaded slides of summer vacations. Most who get serious enough about photography to study the art and craft of it eventually become advanced amateurs or working professionals.

HOW I GOT STARTED IN THE BUSINESS

As a youngster, I had no idea that photography would play a major role in my life and career. My first camera, a Brownie Box, was a gift from my mother on my eighth birthday, in 1951. That summer my family traveled by car to West Virginia to visit friends, and I remember the frightening scenes of devastation along our route, caused by rampaging floods earlier that spring. I photographed the riverside rubble and recorded sights I'd never seen before. My pictures were primitive but photojournalistic nonetheless.

I saw and photographed my first waterfalls on that trip. Two years later we traveled to Canada to visit relatives in Hamilton, Dundas, and Niagara Falls. I shot more waterfalls, whitewater rivers, and Great Lakes ship traffic. To this day, ship shapes and waterscapes remain favorite subjects.

After high school I spent three years with the Army Security Agency. I bought my first 35mm camera then and carried it on all my travels through New England, Alaska, the South, and the Southwest, shooting mostly landscapes and scenics.

My First Sale

In March 1971, twenty years after I shot my first photograph, I was walking near the Chena River in Fairbanks, Alaska, with a camera bag slung over my shoulder. I was a graduate student in English and journalism at the University of Alaska, enrolled in a photojournalism course, and was growing increasingly weary of subzero weather and scenes dominated by snow.

The river had been frozen since early autumn, but sunny skies and temperatures soaring into the teens promised that spring breakup couldn't be far off. As I walked through a small city park, a sign poking askew from a snowbank caught my eye. Black letters warned passersby: KEEP OFF GRASS. I shot it in black-and-white and moved on, looking for more interesting subjects.

Several days later I handed an 8-by-10 glossy of the sign to Chuck Keim, one of my journalism professors. He laughed, then asked, "Where'd you sell it?"

When I told him I hadn't sold it anywhere or even tried, he asked why I had shot the picture. "I thought it was amusing," I said.

"Don't you think others would also find it amusing?" he asked.

"Well, yeah, I guess," I said, but I wasn't convinced. In fact, I felt a little embarrassed walking into the editorial offices of the *Fairbanks Daily News-Miner* to show the print to an editor Professor Keim sent me to see.

"Yeah, yeah, great," the editor said, apparently bored, dismissing me with a sweep of his hand. Unaccustomed to city editors, I mistook his rudeness for rejection. As I turned to head for the door, he called after me, "Give your name and address to the woman at that desk! And your Social Security number! We gotta have your Social Security number!"

I had walked in embarrassed and walked out in disbelief. They had actually bought my simple little picture of a sign sticking out of a snow-bank barely a block away from the newspaper office. There it had stood in its cockeyed protest since the first snows of autumn—for anyone to see, for anyone to photograph. The point is, *I* saw it, *I* photographed it, and *I* got paid for it. The picture ran front page, above the fold, on March 9, 1971. It was the first of many photographs and picture stories I would sell to that newspaper.

Two weeks later spring was on the calendar, but Fairbanks would have none of it. Deep snow had driven hungry moose into the plowed and trampled areas of town and outskirts looking for food. I drove a few miles out of the city in search of picture opportunities. When a young cow moose poked her head through the open passenger window of my pickup truck, I got one shot off before her breath fogged my wide-angle lens.

The resulting print was no prizewinner, but it showed the moose with the outline of the open window and outside mirror clearly behind her head. It was more interesting than my first sale, and I assumed the local daily would want it. When I showed it to Professor Keim and told him what I intended to do with it, he said, "No, this one should go to Anchorage."

He gave me the name and number of someone at the Associated Press, and that afternoon I put the photograph on the next plane out. AP ran it over the wire and paid me ten times what my first sale had brought. I was never again bashful about approaching any editor, art director, or other potential buyer of my photographs.

In Business

That summer, with a course load of only six graduate hours, I was able to freelance part-time. One bedroom of my two-bedroom apartment functioned as an office and studio. The bathroom did double duty as the darkroom.

My professional photographic debut was neither glorious nor glamorous. It was ordinary, mundane. I wasn't winning awards or getting rich, but I was in business.

Until May 1974, when my wife and I left Fairbanks, I continued freelancing—full-time through the summer months and part-time during the academic year.

After a year of traveling through Canada and the United States, we settled on the southern Oregon coast in 1975, in a port town on the sunset slope of the Coast Range. With an endless supply of ships and boats, mountains and waterfalls, beaches and dunes, misty seaports and coastal hideaways, and abundant wildlife everywhere, all my favorite subjects are nearby and daily in my midst.

My home-based business has been a full-time, year-round operation since our arrival in Oregon. I have had to work hard and put in a lot of hours every week, but the tradeoffs have been well worth it. Frankly, it hasn't been terribly difficult.

SHOULD YOU START YOUR OWN BUSINESS?

No one but you can determine whether or not you should start your own photography business, but there are some indicators that might lead you toward the right choice. Of course, if you're not much good at photography and have no interest in getting better, you needn't go any further; find yourself another business. If, on the other hand, you're a competent photographer—even a good one—but have no patience for or interest in managing a business, then check out the help-wanted ads under "Photography," and go to work for someone else.

Even if the notion of being self-employed as a home-based photographer appeals to you and you either possess or are willing to attain the necessary skills, you still need to thoroughly question yourself in order to identify your strengths and weaknesses. This is part of the planning stage, a process that's never too early to start and one that should continue throughout the life of your business.

Following are ten questions you need to answer in as much detail as possible before you start your photography business. So sit down with a pen and pad of paper, and answer as many of these questions as you can. You probably won't be able to respond to all the questions in one sitting. Those left unanswered will guide you toward your weaknesses or the areas where you simply need to do some work or research or perhaps seek help.

Answer the questions as completely and honestly as possible; to do less is to fool yourself and court disaster.

1. *Why do you want to start a home-based photography business?* Provide as many reasons as you can, such as being your own boss, having an

opportunity to spend more time with your family, gaining control over your career, getting out of a dead-end job, avoiding the hassles of commuting, and anything else you can think of.

2. *What photographic experience and management skills can you bring to your new business?* List photographic jobs and management positions you've held, courses you've taken, books you've read—and how each has helped to prepare you. If you identify weaknesses in either photographic experience or management skills, state how you plan to overcome them. If you've never held a management position, perhaps your plan to gain the necessary skills will include launching a research effort at your local library and bookstore, taking business courses at a local community college, signing up for seminars offered by a small-business organization or cooperative, or a combination of these.

3. *How much space will you need for your new business?* First, determine what kind of space you will need: office, darkroom, studio, reception area or waiting room, storage area, library. Every home-based business must have some kind of office. You'll need a darkroom only if you intend to do your own processing. Not every photographer requires a studio, but if you plan to engage in certain kinds of photography, you might. If you specialize in portraiture, you'll need not only a studio but probably some sort of lobby or waiting room for customers as well. Nobody ever has enough storage space. After determining your space requirements, estimate the size in square feet. Sit down with paper, pencil, and ruler and lay out your work area. Allow for furniture and equipment so you'll get an idea of how much space this business is going to take up. (For more information, see Chapter 2 under "Setting Up Your Business Space.")

4. *How do you plan to accommodate the space demands of your new business?* Will you temporarily set up a home office at one end of the dining-room table or put a desk in your bedroom and work there? Nothing wrong with that; many home-based professionals start this way. Will you set up a permanent office in an unused room? Will you work with a temporary darkroom set up in a bathroom, or are you planning a permanent darkroom? Can your office double as a studio, or do you need a separate room? Do you have garage, basement, or attic space you can convert? Can you build on? Everyone will have different

answers to these questions, and for some the answers might change within a short time. Renters are more restricted than owners. Those who rent or own small dwellings are more restricted than those who have plenty of space. If you plan to move within five years, you might do well to list short-term and long-term space considerations. (Chapter 7, "Taxes and Record Keeping," covers the use of a home as a business.)

5. *What are your immediate and future equipment needs and how will you meet them?* List all photographic equipment you will need to start and operate your business for one year: cameras, lenses, tripods, electronic flash units, studio lights and stands, enlarger, and such. List all office and other equipment you will need for the same period: typewriter, computer, telephones, fax machine, copy machine, calculator, filing cabinets, office furniture, and vehicle. Similarly, list your projected equipment needs for five years. In each category, indicate equipment you already own and how you expect to acquire what you don't have. Keep in mind that in addition to acquiring equipment, you'll probably need to update and upgrade some during your first five years of business. (Also see Chapter 2 under "Setting Up Your Business Space.")

6. *What licenses, permits, and laws do you need know to about to operate a business from your home?* Laws vary from state to state, county to county, and city to city. Your state might require you to file your business name with a state agency or to apply for a business or vendor's license. You might have to obtain a permit from your county government. There could be city ordinances regulating the operation of home businesses, even from one neighborhood to the next. You need to know about all such obstacles and how you'll overcome them before you go into business. (Chapter 5, "The Legal Aspects of Your Photography Business," offers more information on zoning ordinances, licenses, and permits.)

7. *How much cash will you need to run your business for one year and where will it come from?* This is no place to fudge the figures. Be honest and as accurate as possible, even though you're making an estimate, and possibly not a very educated one at that. Remember, if you must err on money matters, it's always best to err on the side of fiscal conservatism: Overestimate the payables and underestimate the receivables;

any outcome to the contrary will be a pleasant surprise. Estimate what it will cost you to run the business for a year, and don't forget to include your own salary as part of the cost. Now determine where the operating capital will come from: savings, spouse's income, pension or retirement income, the business itself, or elsewhere. (For more information on financial matters, see Chapters 3 and 4.)

8. *Who are your competitors, how are they doing, and how do you expect to overtake them in the marketplace?* The way you deal with this question depends on the kinds of photography you plan to engage in and how many others work in the same area. If you plan to do family portraits, weddings, and school pictures, you'll be in competition with every other photographer in your community who does the same kind of work. If they're all driving fancy vehicles and living in expensive houses, there's obviously plenty of room for competition. If they're barely scratching out an existence, it could mean the supply is outstripping the demand, and you might need to look for another niche. Chances are, the truth lies somewhere between the two extremes. If you have a particular area of expertise—say, architectural, product, or industrial photography—in a small community, you might be the only photographer so skilled and might well fill a niche. Spend some time with this question, and answer it carefully. This is your first step into the realm of market analysis. (You'll find more marketing information and ideas in Chapter 10, "Marketing Your Photography Business.")

9. *What are the short-term financial and personal goals for your new business?* In other words, what do you expect to earn and accomplish during your first year of operation? This question relates to Question #1 and goes beyond Question #7. Here you need to focus down, get more specific. You should lay out objectives that go beyond mere subsistence or *just getting by.* What are you hoping for? What do you expect your income to be by the end of your first year? Will you have others working for you? What sort of hourly or daily rates or on-location fees will you be demanding by then? How will you have improved or branched out? What will you have learned?

10. *What are your long-term financial and personal goals?* Now discuss everything you covered in Question #9 in terms of a five-year plan. How big do you expect your business to be in five years? How skilled a photog-

rapher do you hope to be? What sort of clientele do you expect to have by then? Will your business continue to grow, or will you want it to level off at some point? Do you plan to hire help? Will you branch out into other aspects of photography? Will you diversify into other areas, such as multimedia productions or desktop publishing? Will you get rich?

AMATEUR VS PROFESSIONAL

Just as there are amateur athletes who are as skilled as or better than their professional counterparts, many serious amateur photographers are every bit as good as most of the people making a living with cameras. The difference has less to do with proficiency than with what photographers choose to do with it.

The distinction used to be a simple one: Amateurs don't get paid for their work; professionals do. That line has been blurred considerably in recent years. While many amateurs are satisfied to treat photography as a hobby, creating images for their own enjoyment and perhaps entering amateur contests to win ribbons and the occasional plum prize, some sell their work to help defray costs. Whether it's a hobby, avocation, or profession, photography is expensive. The materials are costly and the equipment sometimes outrageous in price. As a hobbyist, you might be able to offset some of your expenses by selling your work. As a professional, you'd better be able to sell enough to pay all your expenses and make a decent profit as well.

One of the most attractive aspects of photography is the possibility of advancing from hobby to career, a sequence practitioners of other professions seldom enjoy. We don't see amateur architects, for example, designing skyscrapers and shopping centers for the joy of it, or hobby dentists doing root canals in their spare time. Many photographers, however, work first for the fun of it, then study and master enough techniques to advance to the level of serious amateur, and ultimately put that knowledge and experience to work earning money.

PART-TIME VS FULL-TIME PHOTOGRAPHY

The photographer who decides to work as a home-based professional is faced with deciding between part-time and full-time work. I suspect most of us begin working part-time and gradually or eventually steer our businesses into full-time operations. At least that's what I did, and I recommend you seriously consider doing likewise. There are many advantages to starting part-time. Here are some of the options you can exercise:

- Work part-time at home while retaining a full-time job and its steady income.

- Run a part-time home-based photography business and work at another part-time job to make ends meet.

- Retain the benefits package your employer offers while establishing your home-based business.

- Gain professional experience that will prove invaluable when you go full-time.

- Set up adequate business facilities in your spare time without undue financial strains.

- Gradually invest in photographic and business equipment and furniture.

- See to numerous details at your leisure, such as a logo, business cards, letterhead, and Yellow Pages listing.

- Set up files and establish customer accounts, vendor accounts, and bank accounts.

- Build an excellent credit rating and a solid professional reputation.

- Let your business grow until it's making your projected or required full-time income.

- Build a cash reserve that's big enough to finance your first year's full-time operation.

- Get a feel for the potential of your business and markets before making a major commitment.

You can do all this and more as a part-time home-based photographer. You might continue working part-time indefinitely, until you feel like making it a full-time business. Or you might do as I did: continue caching cash from the income of your part-time business while gaining valuable experience in other, related fields.

I ran my home-based business part-time for nearly four years, enjoying the diversity of the various kinds of work I was involved in, while gaining a tremendous amount of experience in photography and allied fields. By the time I was ready to work full-time at my business, I was making regular sales and earning a fairly steady income. I had established many contacts, set up good working facilities in my home, acquired the equipment I needed, and built good working files and a reference library. I established all the necessary accounts with vendors, banks, and oil and credit-card companies.

Four years of part-time professional photography also enabled me to experiment with a great array of equipment and to gradually acquire more and upgrade what I had. When I started selling photographs in 1971, I owned a Canon FTB single-lens reflex camera with a 50mm lens. By investing my profits in equipment that first year, I added a 28mm lens, a 70-to-210mm zoom lens, a second FTB body, an electronic flash, various filters and lens attachments, two tripods, an assortment of gadgets, and a 6-by-6cm twin-lens reflex camera. I also bought an enlarger, a print washer, a print dryer, and all the tanks, trays, and other equipment I needed to set up a home darkroom.

The following year I started investing in inexpensive studio equipment: copy stand, light stands, photofloods, and backgrounds. I added a 6-by-7cm press camera and also worked with a Hasselblad system for much of the year.

Shortly before leaving Fairbanks in the spring of 1974, I sold all my photography equipment and upgraded to a Nikon system that included three camera bodies, a half-dozen lenses, an electronic flash, and all the necessary filters and gadgets. A year later, when I was preparing to go into business full-time, I bought new darkroom and studio equipment, some secondhand office furniture, and a new IBM Selectric II typewriter. My business was now adequately equipped, but of tantamount importance, my equipment was either new or nearly new, which assured me of good service with minimal downtime.

I paid for everything from the business cash reserve I had accumulated in four years of part-time work, with enough left to cover my first year's expenses and salary. I can't think of a safer, more comfortable way to start a full-time home-based business.

Of course, there is a down side to starting and running a part-time home-based business while trying to hold down a full-time job elsewhere.

It's difficult to do justice to your business while giving your best efforts to an employer. Your first work loyalties must go to that employer, however. It's often a stretch and a hectic way to live and work. But it's also excellent training and might be the only feasible way to realize your dream.

LEARNING THE CRAFT OF PHOTOGRAPHY

I assume that most people planning on going into business as home-based photographers already possess some photographic skills. At the very least, you should have some grasp of basic photographic principles and an abiding interest in learning as much as possible about the profession.

One way to learn is by reading, but if you're new to photography, the last medium you'll want to consult is photographic magazines. They're as readable and valuable to the new photographer as computer magazines are to people looking for a lucid introduction to computers. Unless you already have a fair level of competence and understand the jargon, specialty magazines will be of little value.

Taking Courses

My first recommendation is to take a college-level course in basic photography from a good teacher. I stress: a *good* teacher. The same course can be taught by two different teachers and be as different as *National Geographic* is from *National Enquirer*.

I have taught upper-division college-level photography courses that required students to have had a course in basic photography. I'm always astonished to find a number of students who meet the prerequisites but fail dismally to grasp the most rudimentary photographic principles. I blame their teachers for letting them pass a basic course without understanding such essentials as the shutter-aperture relationship and how film speed is associated with it.

Your first job is to find a course. Then you need to determine the quality and competence of the teacher. You can't be shy. Phone or visit the teacher and ask for a summary of what the course will cover. Tell the teacher what you need and expect from the course, and ask if this course will fulfill those requirements. Find out what texts are to be used, and review them. Talk to the teacher's former students. You should be able to tell within one or two class meetings whether you've found a guru or a bozo. In case of the latter, drop the course, get your money back, lodge a complaint with the school, and look elsewhere for instruction.

Learning by Reading

In the absence of a good basic course, locally available, I recommend a trip to a bookstore or public library. Browse through the photographic titles until you find a book on basic photography that you understand and enjoy. It should be clearly written and well illustrated. Most important, it should provide you with a firm grasp of the elements of photography: shutter speed and aperture, cameras and lenses, film, filters and lens attachments, light and lighting, composition, and the language of photography.

Publishers tend to produce relatively specialized photography books. Often one book will cover a single topic, such as composition, lighting techniques, portraiture, wildlife, action, or shooting for stock. What's more, for most books shelf life is short; what's available now might not be in a year. Consequently, you might have some difficulty finding a good, basic, general text.

When I was on the faculty of the University of Alaska in the early seventies, we had trouble finding a good text for our basic photography course. After trying several, we settled on Ken Muse's *Photo One*. Students seemed to learn more from this than from other texts, perhaps because it is illustrated with cartoons and approaches the subject informally. This book adequately covers the rudiments of photography and introduces readers to darkroom work. If you're an intermediate or advanced photographer, you might find it too elementary.

John Hedgecoe did an admirable job with *The Photographer's Handbook*, which I can happily recommend. While this is a basic, general text, it's a more in-depth work than *Photo One* and contains much that beginning, intermediate, and even advanced photographers will find informative and useful. A good addition to any photographer's library.

The *Kodak Library of Creative Photography* is a general body of photographic information contained in eighteen specialized volumes. Look for this set at a local library, or order it from Time-Life Books. (For more details, consult the Selected Bibliography in the back of this book.)

After a basic course or basic book, you'll be able to read and understand the magazines and more advanced books. You'll have to continue reading magazines and books from then on, not only to learn what you don't yet know but also to keep up with the ever-changing technology.

Workshops and Seminars

You should be able to find workshops and seminars conducted in your part of the country. Some of the traveling schools are excellent sources of information and education. The Nikon School is widely renowned, with weekend courses offered in major population centers every year (see address at the back of this book, under "Courses and Seminars").

Correspondence Study

Correspondence study is another way to learn photography. Some might tell you that the drop-out rate is high among correspondence schools, that correspondence study requires a special kind of person. Indeed, it calls for motivation, self-discipline, and a commitment to learning—identical requirements for anyone who intends to operate a home-based photography business.

The New York Institute of Photography offers a program of correspondence study that gets high marks from those who have investigated or enrolled in it. For details, see the Source Directory at the back of this book, under "Courses and Seminars."

The Optional Apprenticeship

Sometimes it's possible to learn from others, as an apprentice of sorts. If you can stand the low pay and gofer chores, working as a photographer's assistant can be one of the best learning experiences. For that reason, such jobs with big-name photographers are hard to get. Chances are, you'd have to relocate, especially if you live anywhere but in a major metropolitan area.

Learning Darkroom Techniques

I want to emphasize again the value of a good photography course, especially if you want to learn darkroom technique. Any reasonably intelligent person should be able to find the right books to learn camera operation, composition, lighting, and such. You could also learn darkroom equipment and techniques on your own, but you'll learn much faster if someone else shows you the way. Under the tutelage of a good teacher, you'll learn more in a dozen weeks of lecture and lab than you'd pick up in a year or two of reading and teaching yourself.

BRANCHES OF HOME-BASED PHOTOGRAPHY

The home-based photographer can work in any area of photography. You can do wedding, portrait, business and industrial, pet and animal, insurance and legal, medical and scientific, or publication photography. You can sell salon prints through galleries and exhibits or do custom lab work for other photographers. You can work as a freelance photojournalist or do all your work for stock agencies.

You can specialize or diversify. To compete as a specialist—say, in portraiture—you should set out to become the best portrait photographer in your community. If you decide to work in several or many branches of photography, you needn't strive to be, and probably won't be, the best in your community in each branch. You'll have to be good in each, though, and should strive to be outstanding. You might thereby prove yourself the most versatile photographer in your vicinity.

It's important that you have some idea of the direction you want your business to take, and here again planning is crucial. You guessed it: It's time, once more, for the trusty pad and pen. List all the branches of photography you can think of. Identify those that interest you most. If you can, pick the one branch that's most exciting to you; if you can't, don't worry about it.

In this simple exercise you may have already identified the branch of photography you are most suited for and might want to specialize in. On the other hand, perhaps you've discovered that your interests are broad and that you are most inclined toward being a general-assignment photographer.

You needn't set out immediately to specialize in anything, or to generalize, for that matter. You might find in a year or two that you're being pulled one way or another. As long as you continue to stay in touch with your own feelings and ambitions, as long as you continue to plan and set realistic goals, and as long as you continue to strive toward photographic excellence, all that remains is to acquire business acumen.

PHOTOGRAPHER TURNED MANAGER

Being a self-employed photographer has its advantages and disadvantages. One important advantage is that you have the greatest possible control over the business you're involved in because you're the one who's running it. The time and energy required to manage your business, however, is time and energy not devoted to the creative process.

A fact you must face at the onset, before you carry this idea of running your own business any further, is that as a self-employed photographer you will probably spend less time behind a camera than you would working for someone else—serving as staff photographer at a local newspaper, for instance, or as portrait photographer at a major studio. The best you can hope for is that your work will be equally divided between photography and management, so you must have a taste for management.

The photographer who works for someone else need only be good at photography. As the owner of a home-based photography business, you will also have to be a competent manager. In your own business you wear all the hats.

QUICK QUIZ FOR THE HOME-BASED PHOTOGRAPHER

Before getting down to business, as it were, let's see if you've got the stuff to manage your own photography business. Answer *yes* or *no* to the following questions.

	YES	NO
1. Are you a self-starter?	✓	
2. Are you willing to work harder and longer than you ever imagined?	✓	
3. Do you work well without supervision?	✓	
4. Do you work well under pressure?	✓	
5. Are you able to organize details?	✓	
6. Can you take charge of projects and see them through to completion?	✓	
7. Do you have an independent nature?	✓	
8. Do you consider yourself well disciplined?	✓	✓
9. Are you willing to make sacrifices to succeed?	✓	

	YES	NO
10. Do you consider honesty important in business?		
11. Do you assume all your business dealings will be with honest people?		
12. Do you mind seeing to menial chores?		
13. Do you work best as a team member?		
14. Are you a procrastinator?		
15. Do you think work has to be fun?		
16. Are you a creative person?		
17. Can you be stern with people who owe you money?		
18. Do you consider it necessary to meet or beat all deadlines?		
19. Do you have a firm grasp of photographic principles?		
20. Do you own sufficient and adequate photographic equipment?		
21. Do you own as much photographic equipment as you'll ever need?		
22. Do you know as much about photography as you'll ever need to know?		
23. Is the camaraderie of coworkers necessary?		
24. Are strict follow-up procedures a waste of time?		
25. Are peer recognition and praise essential to your success and happiness?		

If you answered *yes* to Questions 1 through 10, *no* to 11 through 15, *yes* to 16 through 20, and *no* to 21 through 25, why aren't you already running your own home-based photography business?

Don't fret if you have some *yes* answers where *no* answers belong, or vice versa. This test was designed to provide a quick self-evaluation and perhaps call to your attention some of the realities of being a self-employed photographer and manager. You might have discovered a weakness or several, areas you need to work on, or attitudes that need adjusting. You have probably also found that you're ready to start seriously thinking about and planning for the grand opening of your new business.

CHAPTER TWO

WORKING OUT OF YOUR HOME

During much of the twentieth century, the trend for most people was to live in one place and work in another. In recent years, however, increasing numbers of people have moved back to their homes to do business. According to the U.S. Small Business Administration, more than 400,000 home-based businesses were launched in 1985. That figure has since more than doubled, to about one million new home-based businesses each year.

Several technological advancements have combined to allow people the increased freedom of working at home. Certainly, the development of the personal computer must lead the list. Reinforcing the computer revolution were the establishment of computer database services, modems for computer-to-computer communication, improvements in telecommunications equipment and telephone services, the introduction of modern facsimile (fax) machines and fax modems, and widespread access to the Internet.

Augmenting all these technological advances was the establishment of nationwide networks of rapid delivery and courier services. The U.S. Postal Service offers Express Mail overnight delivery to most U.S. destinations. United Parcel Service guarantees next-day delivery with its "Red Label" service and second-day delivery of the cheaper "Blue Label" parcels. Similar services are available at competitive prices from other companies, such as Federal Express. It's now possible to send a letter, proposal, report, manuscript, or stack of photographs coast to coast faster than it took to get a document across town twenty years ago.

The attraction of working at home enticed many of us to go into business for ourselves. Working where we live allows us to avoid long, time-wasting commutes and reduces wear and tear on vehicles. We're able to escape the hassles of office politics and personality conflicts with bosses and peers. We can dodge all the nonproductive meetings and work at our own improved pace. We can also arrange flexible schedules to accommodate a variety of needs.

THE PROS AND CONS OF SELF-EMPLOYMENT

For most of us who have been in business awhile, the advantages of home-based self-employment far outstrip the disadvantages. You ought to know at the onset, though, that some people just don't take to this kind of life. So approach your business cautiously, and weigh the options carefully.

I get the impression from people I talk to that the two qualities many people fear they lack are self-motivation and self-discipline. The two attributes work hand in hand and are essential to the success of any home-based business, but these are realities you simply must face, not fears that should unnecessarily put you off. Of course, you must be motivated. Of course, you must be disciplined. But so must you be to hold a job, to get to work on time, to show up for appointments, to take responsibility for projects, to see to family business, to be a dependable person, to be a good friend.

The move from passenger to pilot can seem a quantum leap, but it needn't be frightening. You'll have to reach inside yourself to find the required character traits, but outside influences might be even greater motivators.

When people ask me how I can get up every morning and go to work without giving in to the temptation to sleep in or take the day off and go fishing, I tell them it's easy: I have a natural aversion to poverty, hunger, and failure.

All of us are tempted from time to time, and on rare occasions we even give in. It's human nature, and there's nothing wrong with that. What you can't afford to do, however, is make a habit of succumbing to all the diversions and thereby jeopardize deadlines and other commitments. To do so is to risk your reputation—indeed, your business.

If sleeping in or taking a day or afternoon off might cause you to miss a deadline, then don't do it. If, on the other hand, you've been working hard and your taking a little time off will do no harm, then the decision is up to you. Keep in mind, though, that when you miss a morning, afternoon, or entire day, all your business activities screech to a halt; the work won't get done in your absence. You might have to put in some evenings or weekend time to catch up. So every time you're tempted, ask yourself if it's worth it.

The All-Collar Worker

At a conference I attended a while back, an economist talked about blue-collar and white-collar workers, then told the audience about no-collar workers. "I'm talking about people who wear T-shirts or sweatshirts, Levi's, and running shoes," he said. "They work at home, and they represent the fastest-growing segment of the workforce."

He was referring to more than twenty-five million Americans, or about 20 percent of the entire labor force, who work full-time from their homes. Some are home-based employees of corporations, while the rest of us are in business for ourselves.

Although his facts and figures were interesting, his labeling was all wrong. In our home-based businesses, each of us runs the gamut from chief executive to laborer. I make all the important administrative and creative decisions in my business, but I also order the office supplies, make the coffee, vacuum the carpet, scrub and wax the darkroom floor, sweep up the shop, dust the filing cabinets and bookshelves, put off the filing, and wish someone would wash the windows. If anything, I'm an all-collar worker.

No More Nine-to-Five Grind

Many who aspire toward the independence of running their own home-based businesses dream of the day when they can chuck the daily routine: no more Monday-through-Friday, nine-to-five grind. That's true. Your home-based photography business will probably require a Monday-through-Saturday schedule, with plenty of Sundays thrown in. Instead of slugging away from nine to five, you'll probably be hard at it from six to six and might have to work some evenings to keep up.

No More Bosses

Similarly, those who think being their own boss is the greatest benefit of being self-employed are in for some surprises. The photography business is mainly a service, and when you operate a service business, everybody's your boss. You take orders from art directors, creative directors, and various managers. You do what your customers or clients want you to do. You honor your commitments to countless people, and you meet their deadlines. To do otherwise is to court peril.

Isolation—Curse or Blessing?

Isolation is also something every home-based photographer must deal with. Oddly, the reality of it comes as a surprise to many people who decide to run businesses from their homes. Some are truly distraught by being cut off from daily interaction with others, particularly those who leave busy jobs where isolation is rare or nonexistent. The rest of us revel in the solitude and the high level of productivity it fosters.

If most of your business is local, you will come in contact with more people than if the bulk of your work is for distant clients. Even in the latter case, you'll need to stay in touch with people by phone, mail, fax, and e-mail, and with the occasional business trip, trade show, or association meeting.

If your photography business is one that requires meetings with clients, you might consider luncheon meetings as a way of getting away from home for an hour or so. This can be a refreshing diversion if you don't mind dividing your workday to allow it. Breakfast meetings can be a good alternative for those who don't like to break up their workdays.

If your business is mainly portraiture, weddings, and school photography, or custom lab work, most of your customers will be only casual acquaintances you're not inclined to lunch with. So if you feel the need to get away from your home or to engage in conversation, take a lunch break with a friend or spouse. You might even plan these luncheons to be regular, if not frequent, diversions.

Two self-employed friends of mine who live in Wyoming make it a point to have lunch together once or twice a month as a way of getting out of the house and having a conversation with someone who's not a client or family member. They've gone so far as to set up a lunch fund to which each contributes. That way, no one's responsible for the tab or tip, and it seems then as if neither has to pay for lunch. Little games like this tend to open pressure valves and help make running a business more enjoyable.

SETTING UP YOUR BUSINESS SPACE

One of the first orders of business is to plan, design, and set up your work space. This is a matter of both logistics and legalities. Your business will require a certain amount of space. Your home may or may not impose space restrictions on your business. In order to qualify as a legitimate business for tax purposes, the space you set aside will have to meet certain criteria. (Also see Chapter 7 under "Using Your Home as a Business.")

The advantages of converting part of your home to work space far outweigh the alternative, which is to rent or lease business space. Typically, commercial space rents for a minimum of about $2.00 a square foot per month. You won't burn out brain cells calculating the $300 a month you'll save by converting a 10-by-15-foot spare room into a home office instead of renting downtown.

Just to rent the commercial equivalent of my office, studio, darkroom, and shop would cost me more than $2,300 a month, or nearly four times my monthly mortgage payment. What's more, I get an annual tax deduction for that part of my home devoted entirely to the operation of my business.

How and where you go about setting up your work space is entirely up to you and depends largely on space available and how you intend to operate. Obviously, if you shoot only color transparencies for stock agencies, calendar markets, and card companies, and you send out all your lab work, you won't need a darkroom. If you're strictly a wildlife or travel photographer, or if you shoot only on location, you have no need for a studio.

Every professional photographer, however, needs a place to conduct business: to see to correspondence, accounts payable, accounts receivable, the endless flow of paperwork, and all the other chores of business. Whether this turns out to be one end of the dining-room table, a desk in a corner of a bedroom, or a full-fledged home office depends on what you need and what's available.

One of the beauties of the home-based photography business is that you can start small. Even though photography is relatively expensive at any level, you don't need as much equipment and materials as you might in another kind of business. Consequently, your start-up costs can be comparatively low. Depending on what you already own and how good you are at scrounging and improvising, you should be able to get into business for something between a few hundred and a few thousand dollars—certainly under five thousand.

You need to set up some sort of office space, and there's nothing wrong with using part of another room in your home, except that you may not claim that space as a home office when you file your tax return. Any space you set up in your home for the purpose of running a business must be used regularly and exclusively for that business if you are going to claim a deduction for it. That means it must be a separate room or rooms. If you don't have separate facilities available, so be it.

If you can, though, try to convert any available rooms, add on, or plan for the additional space the next time you move or build. It's better not only for tax purposes, but also for doing business and keeping your business and personal life separate. You will have a discrete, clearly defined place to go to work, to conduct business, and, perhaps most important, to leave at the end of the workday.

As in any other planning operation, you need to put this on paper. You should write out your wants and needs, and sketch out floor plans that will accommodate your physical requirements.

You can operate a photography business from any kind of dwelling. Since my part-time beginnings, I have run my business from an apartment, two log cabins, a townhouse, a rental house, and finally the house I live in now, which was designed to include comfortable living quarters on one level and my business complex on the other.

When I started my business, my wife and I lived in a two-bedroom, one-bathroom apartment. I was able to set up one bedroom as my office and makeshift studio, and I used the bathroom as a temporary darkroom. We had a similar situation at the townhouse we rented when we moved to the Oregon coast.

Although I have been developing and printing all my black-and-white work since 1971, I didn't have an exclusive darkroom set up until 1981, when we built our current house. Nor did I have separate studio facilities until then. I was able to take a tax deduction for the square footage of my home office in our earlier dwellings but not for my temporary darkroom, because it was not used exclusively for business.

There never seems to be enough storage room, so plan accordingly. When we moved into the townhouse, I got along fine for about a year, but then I had to rent additional storage space. When we built the house we now occupy, we planned carefully and thought we'd never run out of space. I'm now considering a major physical reorganization of my business that will probably include the building of a separate storage facility.

In planning the physical structure of your business, pay close attention to your equipment requirements. List your immediate needs for each aspect of your business, and note how you intend to fill them. You might also list your midrange and long-term needs. If you answered the series of questions near the beginning of Chapter 1, you have already made such a list in response to Question 5. Following are some hints that may help you in this process.

The Home Office

The bare essentials for any home office include a desk, chair, filing cabinet, wastebasket, telephone, and typewriter or computer with word-processing software. You will probably want a bookcase or bookshelves and perhaps a storage cabinet of some sort. Most of us need some kind of calculator; I have several small ones stashed here and there and a larger printing calculator on my desk for use with my bookkeeping and accounting chores. To keep track of important names, addresses, and phone numbers, you should have some sort of index—at least an address book but better yet a Rolodex file, or computer software that lets you store and retrieve such information electronically. You'll need a postage scale and at least three file trays or baskets: *in*, *pending*, and *out*. You'll probably find that three aren't nearly enough.

The necessary office tools include pens, pencils, felt markers, ruler, stapler, staple remover, and scissors. You will want at least one tape dispenser; I keep two on my desk: one for transparent tape, one for removable transparent tape.

Required office materials vary from one business to another but certainly include various paper products, staples, paper clips, spring clips, assorted adhesive tapes, mailing and shipping labels, typewriter and printer ribbons, rubber bands, batteries, and file folders.

Paper products I use include scratch pads, Post-it Notes, letter-size ruled pads, computer paper, graph paper, letterhead stationery and envelopes, business cards, 3-by-5-inch index cards, self-adhesive labels in assorted sizes, chipboard and cardboard stiffeners (for protecting photographs in the mail), large mailing envelopes in different sizes, padded mailers, and various printed forms.

You will eventually discover other tools and materials that, while not indispensable, certainly save time, money, effort, or all three. For example, I keep a three-hole punch on my desk and an assortment of rubber stamps.

I also have a Data-Link stamp dispenser, which has a water reservoir and holds a roll of stamps. By placing it on an envelope and pushing downward, the inexpensive little machine dispenses and affixes a stamp in one operation. This may sound like a silly gimmick, but believe me, if you do much business by mail, it will save you a tremendous amount of time. With it I can stamp twenty-five business-size envelopes in about ten seconds. For comparison, see how many you can lick and stick in that time. I bought mine in 1977 when I was working on a project that involved mailing more than 3,000 letters. I've since put thousands of stamps through it, and it still works fine. Look for these dispensers at your local post office, stationery supplier, or print shop.

As any professional photographer does, I use a lot of batteries to power electronic flash units, motor drives, flashlights, tape recorders, calculators, and other gadgets. I switched from alkaline to the rechargeable nickel-cadmium batteries some years ago because they seldom need replacing, save money, and are kinder to the environment when properly discarded. So I keep two battery chargers busy.

Some electronic equipment that requires a lot of power, however, does not function well with ni-cad batteries. Certain motor drives, for example, require more power and operate best with alkaline batteries.

You might find, also, that motor drives and other high-power equipment will stop working before the batteries are fully discharged. Although you will need to replace those batteries, don't discard them, as they may have sufficient power remaining to operate other, less demanding equipment. Test these batteries with a simple, inexpensive battery tester you can buy at your local Radio Shack.

If not an immediate need, a phone-answering machine should at least get high-priority listing. Such machines are available with a wide range of feature options and prices to match. When I bought mine several years ago, I wondered if I would ever need all its bells and whistles. I doubted the worth of a fifty-number memory dialer and considered the speakerphone only marginally useful.

I was wrong. I've managed to fill all fifty slots in the memory dialer, and the speakerphone alone is worth the price of the entire machine for the time it saves. Anyone working with computers knows that phoning a toll-free technical-support number is infuriatingly time-consuming. There are never enough technicians to handle all the calls, so we wait. And wait. And wait. During a recent call, I spent forty-three minutes on hold. By switching on the speakerphone, however, I was able to get on with my work while holding my place in line.

Just as you should plan for more storage space and phone features than you think you'll need, try to design as much horizontal working surface as possible into your home office. Desktops are never large enough, and they act like magnets to clutter. So plan for more surface space than a single desk offers, perhaps with the addition of a worktable, a credenza, or even a second desk.

I have two desks in my office. A conventional desk stands in the middle of the floor, and another behind it functions as a computer station. Other furniture and fixtures in my office include two-drawer and four-drawer filing cabinets, a typewriter stand, a wall of bookshelves, an AM-FM stereo cassette player, and a cuckoo clock for company. Birds of a feather, I guess.

The Home Studio

The studio is probably the most variable room of all among home-based photographers. You may not need one at all, but if you do, you must determine how you will use it in order to know how much space you need and how you will furnish it. My studio would be more than some photographers need but woefully inadequate for many others.

If you do nothing but tabletop and small-product photography, your requirements will be minimal. You may even get by with a small studio arrangement in a corner of your office, as I did for years. If you plan to shoot portraits and family pictures, large objects, or complicated setups, you'll need more space.

The minimum space for portraits should be about 8 feet wide and 10 to 12 feet deep to accommodate backgrounds, lights, and camera equipment. If you intend to specialize in portraits and family pictures, plan for considerably larger dimensions, because you'll need room for bulky equipment and props.

For starters, you'll want some kind of equipment to hold seamless background paper. Simple telescopic stands that extend to 8 feet are probably the cheapest option. For black-and-white photography, the least you'll want is a roll of black and a roll of white seamless. For color and special effects, the choices seem infinite, so you'll need to do some browsing.

For still lifes, tabletop and product photography, demonstration photos, hands-at-work shots, and the like, a setup table or light table works well and needn't cost much. I put together an inexpensive arrangement when I furnished my studio in 1981. It consists of no more than a 3-by-5-foot sheet of ¼-inch tempered plate glass with beveled edges, set atop a pair of sawhorses. With it, I'm able to do all sorts of photography, including shadowless product shots. It's easy to dismantle and move, and it cost me less than $25.

You can also start small and cheap with studio lighting. You'll need a minimum of two lights with stands, but I'd recommend three. Eventually, you'll want to add more for special purposes and tricky lighting. While it's possible to spend $1,000 or more on a single light head, with some careful buying you can put together a three-light outfit with telescopic stands for under $200.

For copy work and some small-item photography, copy stands come with or without integral lighting apparatus. They vary widely in price, from under $100 to $500 or more. You can improvise and make do with a tripod and studio lights, but if you do much copying, invest in a copy stand.

Buy a heavy-duty, 25-foot extension cord. Then fit it with an industrial-grade multi-outlet strip. Get a strip with six outlets, on-off switch, pilot light, and circuit breaker. If you use expensive lights and other electrical equipment in your studio, invest in one of the more expensive multi-outlet strips that includes a surge suppressor.

All that remains to complete your start-up studio is a camera and tripod, which you should already have. Later additions and upgrades will depend on what level of studio photography you hope to achieve.

The Home Darkroom

Whether you're setting up a temporary or permanent darkroom, basic requirements are the same. First, you'll need access to plumbing—hence the popularity of bathrooms and utility rooms as temporary darkrooms. The room must also be light tight or allow for simple measures to make it so.

The ideal room will have no windows, but if the room you must use has one, you need only find a way to shield it. If you're converting the room to a permanent darkroom, use duct tape and heavy-duty aluminum foil to cover the window pane and block out all light. Or you can apply several coats of black paint to the pane until no light penetrates. For temporary purposes, you'll need to make some sort of removable light block you can easily install each time you set up for developing film or making prints.

Doors leak light and must be sealed. In a permanent darkroom, use self-adhesive weather-stripping tape around the door and door jamb. For a temporary darkroom, install a curtain rod inside the room above the door; then hang a black corduroy curtain that's long enough and wide enough to block any light that leaks in around the door. Remove and store the curtain when the room is not in use as a darkroom.

Equipment needs are fairly standard. For developing roll film, you'll need at least one tank and reel, but you'll probably want several. I use Paterson tanks with adjustable film reels that accept 35mm, 120, and 220 film sizes. I find the two-reel and three-reel tanks most useful. You will also need film clips for hanging and drying film.

I store working solutions of film-developing chemicals in one-gallon brown-plastic jugs, one jug each for developer, stop bath, fixer, and rapid-wash hypo-clearing agent. If you save your developer, you'll need another jug for replenisher. You can use any suitable container for storing chemicals, but brown opaque plastic or dark-amber glass jugs or bottles are best, as they block light and retard aging and deterioration.

Other essential film-developing equipment includes a good darkroom thermometer, a lab timer, graduates for measuring and mixing chemicals, a two-gallon bucket, a stirring paddle, a filter funnel, scissors, and an opener for 35mm film (a can-and-bottle opener works fine).

For black-and-white printing, you'll need some kind of containers for storing chemicals. For years, I used the same kind of one-gallon jugs I store film solutions in, but when I built a permanent darkroom, I wanted larger, more convenient containers. I use three two-gallon tanks equipped with spigots, external lids, and internal floating lids to hold developer concentrate and working solutions of stop bath and fixer.

Other necessary printing equipment includes an enlarger, an enlarger timer, safelight(s), a printing easel, three chemical trays, three print tongs, a print washer, and some sort of print dryer. You'll also use some of the same equipment you employ in film developing, such as a thermometer and graduates.

For color lab work, you can use much of the same equipment, but you'll also need some color-dedicated gear, such as a color head for your enlarger and devices to maintain accurate temperature control during developing and processing.

HANDLING GROWTH

There's nothing wrong with modest beginnings. In fact, I'd recommend you start that way. But you must plan to succeed, which means you must plan to expand and to later limit or curtail expansion. In short, you must control the growth of your business.

If you operate your photography business intelligently and aggressively, your business will grow—most rapidly during the first few years. You might also experience rapid growth whenever you branch out into another area of photography. You must pace that growth according to your abilities, resources, and available space.

Eventually, you will be getting all the business you can handle, at which time you must decide whether to level off or continue expanding. This is not as easy a decision as it might at first appear.

Many entrepreneurs equate growth with success and insist that in order to succeed, a business must grow, which is true to some extent. It is, indeed, important for a business to grow during its formative years. It can be dangerous, however, to extend the growth notion too far: to think that the faster a business grows, the more successful it will be; or to believe that if a business doesn't continue to grow, it is destined to fail.

It's actually possible to grow too fast—that is, to take on more than you can handle. If prices quoted to your clients or customers are based on a business run by one person, you can get into serious trouble if you must hire help or farm out work to other photographers to honor your commitments and meet deadlines. This can not only reduce or eliminate your profits but also eat into your operating capital. Your dilemma is that you must either break your promises and miss deadlines or spend extra money to get the work done on time. You can't work that way and expect to stay in business.

Even with proper planning and managed growth, you will eventually reach a saturation point. That's when you will have to decide whether to level off or hire help.

WORKING WITH OTHERS

Sometimes the promise of high profits can cloud vision and impair judgment. There's nothing wrong with providing jobs for others, but you must keep in mind why you wanted your own home-based photography business in the first place. Was it to build an empire or to provide yourself with a satisfying career and comfortable income? In case of the former, you must be willing and able to accept the hassles and responsibilities that come with empire building. If you're among the latter group, you must know how to manage and curtail growth and how to handle potential growth problems.

As your business grows, you might discover that there are times when seven days aren't enough to get the week's work done. A number of factors can contribute to scheduling problems and the need for careful scrutiny of your business's labor requirements.

- *Seasonal aspects.* You might find that there are times of the year when you have more work than you can handle. Portrait photographers, for example, are often busiest just before and during the Christmas holidays. School photography can put strains on your time and resources. Even travel and outdoor photography have seasonal peaks the photographer must consider and learn to deal with.

- *Rush orders.* You won't be in business long before you discover that few customers and clients plan ahead. Everybody, it seems, needs it done yesterday. Even business clients who should know better often end up hiring a photographer at the last minute, almost as an afterthought.

- *Special projects*. From time to time you will probably land jobs outside of or in addition to your usual business. Often these can be lucrative jobs that you can't afford to turn down. Indeed, you might pursue or even initiate them yourself. As well as they might pay, they can put additional demands on your business that call for extraordinary measures.

- *Accumulated chores*. Dealing with all the above problems will force you to set priorities and to put off low-priority tasks until time permits you to address them. These lesser jobs can eventually grow into a major responsibility that must be dealt with.

When faced with these or similar circumstances, you have several choices. Enlisting the help of a family member might be the simplest solution, but this isn't always possible. In my own business, my wife is a great helpmate, especially when we're on the road, gathering photographs and research materials for articles and books. But she has her own full-time career, so she isn't available during the course of a normal workweek.

If you need help with your work and, for one reason or another, no one in your family can come to your aid, you might have to consider hiring help. Your alternatives are to hire personnel on your own or to work with a local employment service.

Often, hiring help only adds to your burdens, and I must recommend you do so only as a last resort. You'll probably need to advertise. Then you'll have to screen and interview prospective employees. In order to attract competent applicants, you'll have to offer a competitive wage and certain fringe benefits.

State and federal regulations make hiring personnel difficult, expensive, and time-consuming. You must pay for unemployment insurance, Social Security, and workers' compensation. You're responsible for deducting Social Security taxes as well as federal, state, and local income taxes from an employee's pay and submitting the deducted funds to the various agencies with all the appropriate forms.

On top of all that, you'll have to pay for a certain amount of nonproduction: holidays, sick days, personal days, and vacation. And you will probably be responsible for some kind of health insurance. The paperwork for all this can be a nightmare, and the cost can reach an amount that is equivalent to between 40 and 45 percent of the employee's pay. If you pay a full-time employee $10.00 an hour, or $400 a week, your actual costs will be in the neighborhood of $14.50 an hour, or $580 a week.

After your business's workload subsides or returns to normal, you'll have to lay off anyone you've hired. This can be a depressing duty for you and certainly an unhappy event for the employee. What's more, it can increase premiums for unemployment compensation insurance.

Hiring Temporary Help

You'll probably be far better off to hire temporary help through an employment service, not to be confused with an employment agency. Employment services are companies that provide workers for other businesses. The employment service tests, screens, hires, and trains the workers; pays their salaries; provides all their benefits; makes all the necessary payroll deductions; and sees to all the necessary paperwork.

Well before you have an actual need, you should find out what sort of temporary help is available in your locale. Check with the local chamber of commerce or Small Business Development Center. Look in the Yellow Pages under such headings as "Employee Leasing," "Employment—Temporary," and "Employment Contractors—Temporary Help."

Most such companies have an employee pool with a wide range of skills in a variety of fields. Most have clerical help and skilled office workers available, and some have people competent in certain specialty areas.

When you use an employment service, you pay an hourly rate to the service, which then pays the employee and keeps a portion for the service. The rate you pay obviously must be higher than what you might pay to an employee you hire yourself, but probably will work out to be a better deal for you in the final analysis.

For example, if the employment service charges you $15.00 an hour for the kind of employee you could have hired directly for $10.00 an hour, this might seem exorbitant at first glance. Consider, however, that your $10.00-an-hour employee will actually cost you $14.50 an hour. So in essence, you end up paying a mere 50 cents an hour to avoid all the time-consuming chores and paperwork associated with advertising for, interviewing, screening, training, and paying an employee.

Independent Contractors

An alternative to hiring help is to use the services of an independent contractor—someone who, like you, is self-employed and works by the job or by the hour, under contract. You and the contractor agree in writing to what the job entails and how much you will pay. The contractor is then responsible for doing the work as stipulated, paying self-employment and income taxes, and filing the necessary forms.

If you use independent contractors in your work, there is one form you might have to file. The Internal Revenue Service requires you to file a Form 1099 for any independent contractor you pay more than $600 during the tax year.

You can advertise for an independent contractor in a local newspaper's classified section, or you can try to find someone through other sources. Put the word out at a local photography dealer's shop or photography club. Another good source is any nearby college or university with a photojournalism or photography program.

When I was at the University of Alaska, we established a photographers' bureau to which anyone could belong by simply signing up and listing days and hours of availability. Most members were students with a wide range of skills. Anyone needing a photographer could phone the bureau and be put in touch with people capable of doing everything from lab work to field work, passport photos to product photography, studio portraits to on-location shoots.

You can hire an independent contractor for any job for which you might otherwise hire an employee. The big difference is that you can avoid most of the headaches and nuisances associated with being an employer.

Collaborating with Others

Collaboration is another way to get help on jobs without hiring employees. In a collaboration you work with one or more other persons to complete a project. For example, you might work with another photographer on a major shoot, or you might work with a writer on a project for publication that requires text and photography. An annual report for a large corporation might require a team of writers, photographers, and illustrators and someone to manage the team and coordinate its efforts.

SEPARATING BUSINESS LIFE FROM PERSONAL LIFE

I have read that it's impossible for the home-based entrepreneur to keep business life and personal life separate. To the extent that no business or job can be kept entirely isolated from personal and family affairs, I would agree. But it's essential for the success of your business and the well-being of your personal life that you make every effort to keep the two distinct and apart.

If you have a family, your home-based business is going to affect it in some way, and vice versa. If your business is only in the preliminary planning stages, waste no time in bringing certain family members on board and making clear to them what your plans are and how they might affect family life. A spouse should be part of your planning from the start. You might want to postpone discussing the venture with young children until you're ready to launch the business, but it might be well to talk with older children early on.

Most important, you must make it clear to your family, friends, and neighbors that although you will be working at home in your new business, you are indeed working, and during work hours you are not available for doing chores, babysitting, playing ball, shopping, running a shuttle service, or doing anything else not related to professional photography.

For some baffling reason, people tend to think that a person who works at home isn't really working. Consequently, you can count on them to try to impose on you in every imaginable way. Friends, neighbors, and even family members will think nothing of phoning or dropping in during business hours just to chat, when they would never dream of doing such a thing to a plumber, lawyer, or carpet installer who works away from home.

Sometimes home-based entrepreneurs get what they ask for—no respect. I've heard of some who delight in the fact that they're able to work at home all day in robes and slippers. I can't imagine taking my business seriously, or expecting others to, while lounging around all day in bed clothing. I certainly can't entertain or meet with clients so attired. And what are drop-ins and coffee klatschers to think if I greet them at the door in pajamas and try to convince them I'm busy?

Of course, I might catch up on paperwork late at night in the bedroom. I often see to early-morning phone calls with my first cup of coffee, before I've showered and donned my work duds. When it's time for business, however, I'm dressed for it.

It's also important for your business image and peace of mind that you establish a business routine. You must have operating days and hours, and you must make these known to family, friends, and neighbors. Otherwise, they'll be all too quick to assume you're not really working.

CHAPTER THREE

FINANCIAL PLANNING

n the broadest sense, the operation of any business can be divided into two basic categories: the management of money and the management of time. Although the two are inextricably intertwined, you should first expend your efforts toward planning and managing financial matters.

For most people, starting a new business involves a great deal of guesswork. I suspect that's one reason so many small businesses soon end up in financial difficulty. As I said earlier, the home-based photographer has the distinct advantage of being able to operate part-time before starting a full-time business. The ability to analyze revenues and expenditures from the part-time business and extrapolate them to reflect full-time operation removes much of the speculation and makes financial planning more accurate and management much easier.

Even if you start your business on a part-time basis, you must not treat it as a hobby. I suspect that most photographers who decide to set themselves up in business were first serious amateurs who sold enough work to buy photography equipment and materials and offset the costs of an expensive hobby. A business—part-time or full-time—must do more than that. It must generate sufficient revenue to cover expenditures and make a profit.

It's never too soon to begin planning and managing finances. If you're a hobbyist looking forward to turning your hobby into a business, begin keeping good records immediately. Learn exactly what everything costs, and keep track of price increases. Conduct time studies to learn how long it takes you to do everything associated with photography. Then look for ways to cut costs and reduce time.

START-UP COSTS

Before launching your business, you need to estimate what it will cost you. If you have kept good records of your amateur activities, estimating start-up costs should prove much easier. Nevertheless, it will still require some guessing, albeit guessing based on experience.

Even if you have never bought a new car and know little or nothing about cars, it's easy to learn approximately what such a purchase will cost you. You simply do a little research, shop around, compare various makes and models, decide what features you need and what you can get by without, then negotiate the best deal possible. By the time you're ready to buy, you will know exactly what the car of your choice will cost you.

Some new entrepreneurs expect the start-up costs of implementing a new business idea to be as straightforward and clear cut. Sadly, they are not. There is no way you will determine the exact costs of running a business until you're running it, and even then you must stay alert for potential surprises.

If that sounds like a risky Catch-22, you have grasped the concept. You can greatly reduce the risks and improve the accuracy of your estimates, however, by keeping good records as an amateur and then as a part-time professional.

You'll find that not all the projections, statements, and reports the accountants, consultants, and business writers insist we use are of equal value to all businesses; some are downright useless. Even those that are useful operating tools for running your business can be of little or no value in the start-up process.

In the pages that follow, however, you'll find some tips that will steer you in the right direction and help you to realistically estimate what starting a new business might cost you.

Schedule of Estimated Start-up Costs

One document you will need is a schedule of estimated start-up costs. This is no more than a list of all the equipment, materials, supplies, and expenses associated with running your home-based photography business. Compiling the list will force you to dwell on important details you might otherwise ignore, such as what insurance is going to cost you, how much film you'll have to stock, what your phone and utilities will cost—in short, how expensive this business is going to be. The total of all these costs will be the start-up target you'll need to aim for as you plan your business.

Most of the business guides I've reviewed recommend that new entrepreneurs have at least three months' operating capital before launching a new business, and few mention anything about the owner's salary. You will certainly want to include your salary as part of any start-up projection you make. What's more, you ought to have more backing you than a mere three months' worth of funding for a full-time business.

I ran my business part-time until I had a year's salary and expenses in the bank, and all the while I was investing in and upgrading equipment. By the time I was ready to go full-time, my business was in good shape, and I was able to run it without many financial worries. I suggest you take a similar route, and make sure you have at least six months' salary and operating capital backing you.

OPENING BANK ACCOUNTS

I've read a number of publications that insist the first thing an entrepreneur do is head for a bank and open a business checking account. The authors warn that you must never use a personal checking account for business purposes. One reason given is that business and personal accounts must be kept separate for bookkeeping and tax purposes. Another is that vendors and others you deal with won't think much of you if you pay with personal checks. What utter nonsense!

So what is the home-based entrepreneur to do at bill-paying time—write personal checks for the home or personal portion of the electric bill and auto insurance, then write business checks for the business portions? What a bookkeeper's nightmare that would be.

As one who has been managing some kind of business—either mine or somebody else's—for nearly thirty years, I know that nobody cares one whit about being paid with a personal check instead of a business check, providing there are sufficient funds in the account. My wife and I have

ESTIMATED START-UP COSTS

1. Decorating and remodeling $ _____

2. Furniture and fixtures $ _____

3. Office equipment $ _____

4. Photography equipment $ _____

5. Vehicle $ _____

6. Insurance $ _____

7. Licenses and permits $ _____

8. Legal and professional fees $ _____

9. Office supplies and materials $ _____

10. Photography supplies and materials $ _____

11. Stationery and business cards $ _____

12. Advertising $ _____

13. Unexpected expenses $ _____

TOTAL ESTIMATED START-UP COSTS $ _____

written more than 10,000 checks on the account we're now using. A creditor is going to worry a lot less about my personal check #10864 than business check #11 from some outfit that's been operating for about a month.

More than one publication suggests that aspiring entrepreneurs can shake the onus of the obviously new business checking account by ordering checks that begin with higher numbers. In other words, instead of a sequential check-numbering system that begins with check #1 or #101, you should direct the printer to start with #1001 and put something over on suppliers and others whose products and services you purchase. But anyone who thinks this ruse has escaped the attention of vendors and their credit managers is naive. What's more, credit managers set up new accounts after running credit investigations, so credit will be extended to you before anyone has seen the color of your money.

If you already have a personal checking account, use it. If not, set one up. If you prefer a business checking account, that's all right, too, but don't establish one for the wrong reasons.

I do recommend that you set up a separate business savings account rather than use a personal savings account for business. The extra account won't cost you anything and will make it easy to keep business funds separate. An alternative is to skip the business savings account and open an interest-bearing checking account for your business. Visit a number of banks and learn what they offer. Then establish the kind of account that provides the most and costs the least.

My wife and I have a joint checking account that I've been using for business since 1975. I have had a savings account for my business at the same bank for just as long. We also have a personal savings account at another bank. Both banks have branches less than a mile from our home.

Don't let the cost of an account be your sole guiding influence. Consider the importance of convenience and simplicity. For example, several banks in the community where I live offer lower monthly service charges than I pay. At one, I could save $1.00 a month but would not enjoy the convenience of a drive-up window. At another, I'd save $2.00 a month but would have to drive thirty minutes out of my way, wasting two hours each month. Time is tantamount to money in any business, and it pays to manage both wisely.

THE PERSONAL FINANCIAL STATEMENT

Do you know what you're worth? Your creditors may want to know, and any institution you approach for a long-term loan certainly will. To answer the question, you should prepare a personal financial statement, also known as a statement of financial condition, or statement of net worth.

This is a relatively simple form with two columns. To prepare it, start by creating a form with your name, address, and phone number centered at the top of the page.

PERSONAL FINANCIAL STATEMENT

Name _____

Address _____

Phone _____

ASSETS		LIABILITIES	
Cash	_____	Accounts Payable	_____
Checking Accounts	_____	Contracts Payable	_____
Savings Accounts	_____	Notes Payable	_____
Stocks	_____	Taxes Payable	_____
Bonds	_____	Real Estate Loans	_____
Securities	_____	Vehicle Loans	_____
Real Estate	_____	Other Liabilities	_____
Vehicles	_____		
Accounts Receivable	_____		
Other Liquid Assets	_____		
TOTAL ASSETS	_____	**TOTAL LIABILITIES**	_____

NET WORTH _____
(assets minus liabilities)

In the left column, list all your assets: cash, checking accounts, savings accounts, real estate, stocks, bonds, securities, and accounts receivable. Also list such assets as vehicles and equipment that have cash value after allowing for depreciation. When you add up this column, you arrive at a figure representing your total assets.

In the right column, list all your liabilities: accounts payable, contracts payable, notes payable, taxes payable, real estate loans, and anything else you owe. When you add up this column, you arrive at a figure representing your total liabilities.

Create a line for net worth. Subtract your total liabilities from your total assets, and enter the result as your net worth.

Keep this statement on hand, and update it periodically—at least every year. You will probably want to include it as part of your business plan (covered in Chapter 6).

COLUMNAR PADS FOR ACCOUNTING AND BOOKKEEPING

Accountants usually prepare various statements on columnar pads, the common sizes of which range from 8½-by-11 inches to 14-by-17 inches and include versions with three, four, six, eight, thirteen, and fourteen columns. Use whatever size and format of columnar pad works best for you, but be advised that the outsize, unwieldy pads are a nuisance to store.

For a number of reasons, I use one size and style of pad for all my accounting and bookkeeping: a vertical-format, four-column pad that measures 8½-by-11 inches. The format and standard letter size make such pads compatible with all my documents and files. They adapt handily to any application. I use them for making monthly, quarterly, annual, midrange, and long-range studies and projections, as well as for all my income-tax records. What's more, I need only stock one size, so I order them a dozen 50-sheet pads at a time, thus markedly reducing my per-pad price.

PROFIT-AND-LOSS PROJECTIONS AND REPORTS

A profit-and-loss statement (often called a P&L) is an accounting document that measures or predicts your business's operation in terms of net sales or fees, less expenses and other costs, to create an accurate profit picture or reasonable profit prediction. By definition, this document increases in management value with the life of the business, because its degree of accuracy depends on profit history. As defined, it's of marginal value for many start-up businesses.

You can make this a useful management tool if you will follow my recommendations and forgive my nagging. Keeping accurate records of all transactions during your amateur and part-time days, and logging all the hours you spend working at the business of photography, will create a profit history that you can use to make accurate projections for your full-time business.

The columnar pad commonly recommended for P&L statements is of horizontal format, with a 3-inch-wide vertical column on the left and thirteen narrow vertical columns across each page. To enter both estimated and actual figures for each month and the year-end totals, you can scribe a vertical line down the center of each narrow column, creating twenty-six columns in all.

In my system I forgo the ability to scan twenty-six columns on a single page, but I gain much more in the way of readability. Instead of a single statement that reflects estimated and actual figures, I prepare two separate documents: a P&L projection for estimated figures and a P&L report for actual figures.

You will probably find that the calendar year works best as your business's fiscal year. Unless you start your business in January, though, the first months of operation will constitute a partial year. After that, however, you can do all projecting, calculating, bookkeeping, and reporting according to the standard January-to-December calendar.

If you use the four-column pads, your profit-and-loss projection for the first full year will take four pages. On the first page create a column each for January, February, March, and First Quarter. Subsequent pages will reflect income and expenses for the remaining months and quarters.

The second-year P&L projection will require one page, with one column devoted to each quarter. Add a line at the bottom of the page for the year-end total. Add the totals for the four columns and enter the profit or loss as the year-end total.

For the long-range P&L projection, use one page with a column each for third-year, fourth-year, and fifth-year totals.

PROFIT-AND-LOSS PROJECTION/REPORT
(Estimated/Actual)

	JANUARY	FEBRUARY	MARCH	FIRST QUARTER TOTALS
REVENUE				
Services				
Merchandise sales				
TOTAL REVENUE				
COST OF GOODS SOLD				
Materials and supplies				
Outside labor				
Shipping				
Miscellaneous				
TOTAL COST OF GOODS SOLD				
GROSS PROFIT				
EXPENSES				
Wages/salaries				
Payroll deductions				
Advertising				
Vehicle				
Depreciation				
Insurance				
Interest paid				
Legal & professional fees				
Office				
Rent/lease				
Repairs & maintenance				
Supplies				
Permits & licenses				
Travel & entertainment				
Utilities				
Telephone				
Postal				
Dues & publications				
Printing & copying				
Trash collection				
Miscellaneous				
TOTAL EXPENSES				
NET PROFIT (LOSS)				

In the left column of the P&L projection, under Revenue, list income from sale of services and merchandise on separate lines. Add the two, and enter a figure for Total Revenue.

Under Cost of Goods Sold, list amounts paid for materials and supplies, outside labor, shipping, and miscellaneous costs. Add this column, and enter a figure for Total Cost of Goods Sold.

Subtract Total Cost of Goods Sold from Total Revenue, and enter the result as Gross Profit.

Under the heading of Expenses, list wages (including any salary you extract from the business), payroll deductions (if you have employees), and all overhead and other expenses associated with operating your business. Add this column, and enter the sum as Total Expenses.

Subtract Total Expenses from Gross Profit, and enter the result as your projected or estimated Net Profit (Loss) for that accounting period.

As you progress through your first full year of business, prepare a profit-and-loss report at the end of each quarter. These reports should be identical in form to the P&L projections, except that they should reflect actual instead of estimated numbers. Comparing the P&L projections with the P&L reports should help you make more precise estimates in the future and more accurate midrange and long-range projections.

Use your first-year P&L projection as your operating budget. At the end of your first full year of operations, use your P&L reports to adjust your projections and create a month-by-month projection and budget for the upcoming year.

In effect, after your first year of business, the second-year projection then becomes the first year in your five-year profit-and-loss projection. That is, at the end of each year, you should create a new P&L projection for five years, following the same format as your original P&L projection.

BALANCE SHEETS

A balance sheet is so named because the assets listed in the left column should equal the liabilities in the right column plus the owner's equity. It's a fairly useless document for new businesses and may be of only marginal value for many sole proprietors (see Chapter 5 for a definition of "sole proprietor"). It might prove useful, however, if you need to seek

BALANCE SHEET

ASSETS

Cash (bank accounts): $ _____

Accounts Receivable: _____

Inventory (if applicable): _____

Prepaid Expenses: _____

Short-Term
   Investments: _____

**TOTAL CURRENT
   ASSETS** $ _____

LONG-TERM INVESTMENTS

Land $ _____

Buildings (cost): _____

Less Depreciation: _____

Net Value: _____

Equipment (cost): $ _____

Less Depreciation: _____

Net Value: _____

Furniture/Fixtures: $ _____

Less Depreciation: _____

Net Value: _____

Vehicles (cost): $ _____

Less Depreciation: _____

Net Value: _____

TOTAL FIXED ASSETS $ _____

OTHER ASSETS $ _____

TOTAL ASSETS $ _____

LIABILITIES

Accounts Payable: $ _____

Short-term Notes: _____

Amount Due on
   Long-term Notes: _____

Interest Payable: _____

Taxes Payable: _____

Payroll: _____

**TOTAL CURRENT
   LIABILITIES** $ _____

**OWNER'S
   EQUITY** $ _____
(assets minus liabilities)

**TOTAL LIABILITIES
   & EQUITY** $ _____

Current Date: _____

financing, so you ought to know what it is and how to create one. Of all the analytical and forecasting documents, the balance sheet is the least useful and informative for the home-based photography business.

Balance sheets are usually prepared at the end of the year. The so-called pro forma balance sheet is one prepared in advance of the coming year or accounting period and is hypothetical in nature.

CASH-FLOW PROJECTIONS AND REPORTS

Cash flow is more than net profit; it's how money moves into and out of a business. It covers all business income and cash reserves after expenditures and can indicate the timing of cash movement.

For your business to succeed, it's essential that you ensure a steady and substantial income, not only to pay business expenses and to buy materials and equipment but also to provide you with an adequate personal income and benefits.

You must keep track of cash flow by regular reporting of income and expenditures. In most businesses this is done monthly, with quarterly and yearly totals included. Accurate and timely records will enable you to track cash flow and forecast future needs and trends, which will allow you to make intelligent capital investments and ward off potential problems or interruptions of cash flow.

Cash-flow projections and reports are similar in form and format to profit-and-loss projections and reports. In fact, they're similar in content, but with two important exceptions. Profit-and-loss projections and reports are designed to provide estimated and actual net profits before taxes, and they do not include cash-reserve information. Cash-flow projections and reports provide estimated and actual after-tax profits plus available cash reserves to indicate a cash position at the end of an accounting period: month, quarter, year.

To prepare a cash-flow projection for one year, you can use a sheet from a thirteen-column pad, or four sheets from a four-column pad, as I do. As with the P&L projections and reports, every four-column page provides a column each for three months and one column for quarter totals.

In the left column Item 1 should be Cash on Hand as of the first of the month. This includes any amount of currency earmarked for business purposes, as well as amounts in any business bank accounts.

CASH-FLOW PROJECTION/REPORT

	JANUARY	FEBRUARY	MARCH	FIRST QUARTER TOTALS
1. CASH ON HAND (first of month)	_____	_____	_____	_____
2. CASH RECEIPTS	_____	_____	_____	_____
a. Cash Sales	_____	_____	_____	_____
b. Collected Receivables	_____	_____	_____	_____
c. Other	_____	_____	_____	_____
3. TOTAL CASH RECEIPTS	_____	_____	_____	_____
4. TOTAL CASH AVAILABLE	_____	_____	_____	_____
5. CASH EXPENDITURES				
a. Gross Wages	_____	_____	_____	_____
b. Taxes	_____	_____	_____	_____
c. Materials	_____	_____	_____	_____
d. Supplies (office, etc.)	_____	_____	_____	_____
e. Services (lab, etc.)	_____	_____	_____	_____
f. Repairs & Maintenance	_____	_____	_____	_____
g. Advertising	_____	_____	_____	_____
h. Vehicle	_____	_____	_____	_____
i. Travel & Entertainment	_____	_____	_____	_____
j. Accounting & Legal	_____	_____	_____	_____
k. Rent	_____	_____	_____	_____
l. Telephone	_____	_____	_____	_____
m. Utilities	_____	_____	_____	_____
n. Insurance	_____	_____	_____	_____
o. Printing & Copying	_____	_____	_____	_____
p. Postage	_____	_____	_____	_____
q. UPS, Fed Ex, etc.	_____	_____	_____	_____
r. Dues & Publications	_____	_____	_____	_____
s. Miscellaneous	_____	_____	_____	_____
t. Other	_____	_____	_____	_____
u. Subtotal	_____	_____	_____	_____
v. Capital Expenditures	_____	_____	_____	_____
6. TOTAL CASH PAID (u. plus v.)	_____	_____	_____	_____
7. CASH POSITION (4 minus 6)	_____	_____	_____	_____

Item 2 is Cash Receipts for the month, itemized as cash sales, collected receivables, and any other receipts, including any cash infusion, as from your business savings, the sale of capital equipment, or any other source.

Item 3 is Total Cash Receipts. Add Item 1 and Item 3, and enter that figure as Item 4: Total Cash Available.

Item 5 is Cash Expenditures. Under that heading, itemize and list all cash that your business had to pay out during that accounting period, including all wages (yours and any others'), all taxes, all expenses and overhead. You can modify this listing to suit your needs. In my own cash-flow projection, I have itemized subheads alphabetically listed from *a* to *v*.

Item 6 is Total Cash Paid, the sum of everything listed under Cash Expenditures. Subtract Item 6 from Item 4, and enter the result as Item 7: Cash Position.

At the end of any accounting period, when Total Cash Available is greater than Total Cash Paid, a positive figure will represent your Cash Position. If Total Cash Paid is greater than Total Cash Available, your Cash Position will be a negative figure, also referred to as negative cash flow.

The purpose of the cash-flow projection is to identify any negative cash position so you can take action to rectify the situation.

As with the profit-and-loss documents, you should also prepare a cash-flow report, which is identical to the cash-flow projection except that it reflects actual instead of estimated figures. Regularly comparing the two documents helps you become more accurate in your forecasting.

As I write, the calendar is running out, but I have not yet taken time to prepare a cash-flow projection for next year. Nevertheless, I know that, barring unforeseen catastrophe, my most troublesome months will be June and December. They have been for well over ten years and will likely continue to be. For the past five years, November has been my third most expensive month, and May has come up a close fourth.

Not only can I predict which months might slip into a negative cash position, but I also know why. In June and December, in addition to all the usual expenses, I have several hefty semiannual and annual bills to pay—mainly insurance premiums. Also, spring and fall are my busiest seasons for outdoor and travel photography, so I'm on the road a good bit then. I always charge my fuel and motel bills to credit cards. I use a lot of film then and must constantly replenish my photographic supplies. It can take from thirty to sixty days for all these charges to show up on my credit-card bills. Those arriving earliest are usually due in May and November, but the bulk of them end up in my accounts-payable file in June and December.

Fifteen years ago I couldn't have made such predictions as I just have. But by preparing certain useful projections and reports and paying attention to how cash moves through my business, I can now do a pretty good job of forecasting trends. Consequently, I'm able to use all these figures to my best advantage—whether to tighten my purse strings to see my business through some lean days or to make a timely capital investment.

Cash-flow analysis can be much more complicated and usually is for larger, more complex businesses. Sadly, some writers, consultants, and educators insist the topic be as cumbersome and confusing for owners of small businesses. They tend to make it an academic exercise that serves little practical purpose for the home-based photographer. Try to keep it as simple as possible.

CREDIT AND BORROWING

Although many entrepreneurs start businesses on borrowed capital, I want to warn you away from this practice. Instead of borrowing start-up cash, work part-time, invest in equipment, and build a substantial savings account before launching your full-time business. Don't start with long-term debt.

Short-term debt is another matter, and it takes many shapes. Every time you pay for a tank of gas with an oil-company credit card, you aren't really paying for it but instead are putting off payment until the company sends you a bill. Likewise with the motel bill you put on an American Express card, the film order you charge to a Visa account, or the lens you put on a MasterCard. When you charge office and photography supplies and materials to accounts you have established with vendors, you also take on short-term debt.

This form of borrowing not only is an acceptable practice but when properly managed can offer a number of advantages. Credit cards and vendor accounts can be a great aid to bookkeeping. They eliminate the need to keep large amounts of cash on hand and reduce the number of checks you have to write.

They also speed up delivery of mail orders, because your supplier can ship immediately instead of waiting for a check to clear. If you run into a problem with a supplier, you stand a better chance of getting quick satisfaction if you charged your order to a credit card—such as Visa, MasterCard, or American Express—because your credit-card company will contact the supplier on your behalf, which not only saves you time and trouble but also exerts more pressure on the supplier than you could ever hope to.

If you can avoid the expensive trap of revolving credit and pay all your credit-card and other accounts in full as the bills arrive, you will soon build a good credit rating that will serve you well if you need to seek long-term financing. Even if you adopt the policy of avoiding long-term debt, you might sometime face the need to borrow for your business. For example, you might have to replace an expensive piece of photographic equipment, upgrade a computer system, or buy a new vehicle. Sometimes it's impossible to make such high-ticket purchases without a long-term loan.

You might also land contracts that force you to borrow for capital investment. For example, doing the best and most cost-effective job might hinge on your owning certain equipment—perhaps an expensive lens or another camera body. Or it could be that just as you are trying to get a few more months' use out of your business vehicle, you land a job requiring considerable travel. These are times when borrowing now could pay off handsomely later.

Under such circumstances, be sure to shop around for the best interest rates. Before you visit bankers, head for your local Small Business Development Center or write to the U.S. Small Business Administration for information on SBA loan programs, such as the guaranteed-loan program, export revolving line of credit, and small-loan program. The Small Business Development Center can alert you to any other state and federal programs for which you might qualify. Among the most common are special loans for veterans, women, and members of minority groups.

Everybody in America who has a credit history is in the computer files of at least one credit-reporting company. It can cost $25 or more for a single report from one of these companies, but you are entitled to one copy of your own credit report free of charge, except for a small handling fee. Your bank should be able to handle the transaction, and I recommend you make this a top priority.

Many people have complained about errors in their credit reports that have caused them trouble getting loans. You need to examine your own credit report to determine your credit rating and the accuracy of information in your report. If you find errors, get them corrected immediately; they can affect your credit rating and interfere with your ability to secure financing.

CHAPTER FOUR

FINANCIAL MANAGEMENT

There is no magic formula for answering that most popular of questions, "How much should I charge for my products or services?" I can no more tell you what to charge your customers than a bed-and-breakfast innkeeper in Fargo could tell a hotel owner in San Diego how to set rates. Both might be in the lodging business, but beyond that, there are simply too many differences and variables.

Local cost of living is a major determinant. It's far cheaper to do business in North Dakota than in California. Even one part of a state can differ greatly from another. In northern California you can still find a clean, comfortable, modern motel room for under $45 a night; in southern California I've seen RV spaces for $45 a night.

Every business is different. One photographer might specialize in weddings and augment his business with graduation and family portraits. Another might work exclusively as a scenic photographer, selling mainly to calendar and postcard companies. Yet another might be a freelance photojournalist who also sells work through stock agencies. One rural-based photographer might traipse alone through forests, meadows, mountains, and river bottoms, satisfied to gross $200 a day photographing wildlife. His big-city counterpart might engage only in glamour photography, employ several assistants and a secretary, and charge $1,000 or more a day, plus expenses.

Only you can determine what to charge for your services or products, so you will have to do your homework. Although there are books and associations that can help you tremendously, in the end your pricing policy will be based on what area or areas of photography you work in, how you operate, how you stack up against the competition, where you sell your work, and where you do your work.

No matter what aspect of photography constitutes your main business interest, you'll have your work cut out for you in the initial pricing process. You will also find that you must constantly monitor costs and competition so you will know when and how much to increase prices.

In some fields of photography, such as shooting for stock agencies or working as a freelance publication photographer, you will have little or nothing to do with setting prices. When the stock agency sells rights to one of your images, you will get your share of what the agency was able to charge. In the case of periodical and book publishers, you will get paid that publisher's going rate, unless you negotiate something else prior to submission.

Portrait photographers seem to have the most enviably easy job of pricing. Most calculate their cost of doing business and try to translate that into specific prices for different size prints, usually with price reductions for each subsequent print made from the same negative. The rationale here is that most of the work goes into producing that first print—setting up and shooting the portrait, developing and handling the film, enlarging, and making the print. After the first print is made, turning out a duplicate requires little more than making an identical enlarger exposure and processing the print.

Some portrait photographers charge a sitting fee, which covers all phases of the portrait, up to the point of making the print. Then they charge the same for each print made, no matter how many are ordered.

In certain kinds of photography, the day rate is common. For me, this has proved the best way to bill my time for on-location photography, such as for advertising, brochure or catalog illustration, and even publication photography that is financed by a client.

Some publishers' rates are so low I can't afford to work for them, but if the publisher can entice a company to subsidize the job, I usually end up making top rates and the publisher gets a package from an experienced professional. For example, several years ago, when a timber-industry trade journal wanted an illustrated article on some huge off-road log trucks used on sprawling tree farms owned by one of the nation's biggest timber companies, I got the job, but not from the magazine. The timber company's public relations director hired me, provided a vehicle, assigned a company supervisor to escort me during the location work, and paid my day rate and expenses.

PRICING FOR PROFIT

Before establishing your own prices, you will have to determine what kinds of photography you will be doing; then research those areas to determine how payment is commonly made and what it amounts to. If you plan to operate a portrait studio from your home, find out what other portrait studios in your area are charging. This will provide a basis for your pricing structure—a figure to work with. Then determine how you fit into the community of local portrait photographers.

You don't want to start out as the most expensive photographer in town; nor should you be the cheapest. If your pricing is midrange, you can gradually increase it as your reputation for quality and reliability grows. Even if you are able to work considerably cheaper than other photographers in your locale, undercutting their prices might work against you in two ways. First, your low prices will turn away some potential customers who reason that you get what you pay for. What's more, your low prices might invite your competitors to retaliate.

In my business, income derives primarily from publishers' going rates, royalties, my day rates, hourly jobs, and flat fees. Obviously, I've had to spend considerable time analyzing my costs and factoring in my required salary to determine how much profit I need to make. You'll have to do the same.

Setting Rates

If you plan to do any on-location shooting, you will need to set up some sort of a rate structure for that. Many, if not most, location photographers charge day rates. Some also have half-day rates. My rate structure includes hourly, daily, and weekly rates. I also break my fees into three categories: local, state, and national.

To anyone who's familiar with the day rates of most big-city photographers, mine must seem paltry. Many charge for a day what I get for a week. But I live in a small community on the southern Oregon coast. The population of my entire county is about 50,000. The cost of living is lower here than, say, Portland or Seattle, where the day rates might run two to five times what I can command.

For local clients, I charge $45 an hour, $300 a day, or $1,200 a week. If a job takes me to a nearby town but I can finish the location work and return home the same day, I charge my local rate. If the job requires overnight lodging but is still in the state, I charge my state rate: $55 an hour, $400 a day, or $1,500 a week. For all out-of-state work, I bill my time at $70 an hour, $500 a day, or $2,000 a week.

You might wonder why I list hourly rates for anything but local work, since it's obvious that I can't get any out-of-town job done that fast. I use hourly instead of half-day rates for small jobs and to calculate overtime. Some photographers bill their time according to a day rate, based on an ordinary eight-hour workday. When the client or the nature of the job requires shooting from sunrise to sunset, the photographer then adds a half-day to his day rate to cover the extra time.

When a local client asks me to quote a small job, I say that I get $45 an hour, for a minimum of four hours, which means if the job takes only an hour or two, I still charge for four. So why not a half-day rate? Figure it out. Half of my day rate is $150; four hours at $45 an hour is $180.

I'm also able to tell clients that I bill by the hour, day, or week, whichever is cheaper for the client. Eight hours at my local hourly rate is $360, so $300 a day is cheaper. Five days at $300 would be $1,500, but I charge local clients only $1,200 a week.

I charge overtime for anything over eight hours in any day and for all weekend work. I base the overtime on the applicable hourly rate and calculate it at time and a half (hourly rate x 1.5 = overtime rate). So my local, state, and national overtime rates are $67.50, $82.50, and $105.00 an hour, respectively. I do this as much to discourage overtime as to collect larger fees.

I charge all rates portal to portal, plus mileage or travel expenses, materials, and operating expenses. To cover food and lodging, I let the client choose between paying my actual expenses or per diem of $125.

Expenses

I used to absorb a lot of costs that seemed minor—such as film for small jobs, the cost of chemicals, and expenses associated with packing and shipping—but I have changed that policy. One reason is that these seemingly incidental costs have increased markedly in recent years. Also, I've paid enough bills to the practitioners of law and medicine to know that these folks charge for every paper clip and Band-Aid.

Overhead

If you're charging by the hour or the day, in addition to charging for the materials and expenses directly related to a particular job, you must also charge for the overhead cost: rent, utilities, office supplies, depreciation, and anything else that's not a direct material or labor cost. Of the several ways to calculate the overhead rate, the simplest and most sensible is to derive an hourly rate. You can do this as a part-time or full-time photographer, providing you keep track of all your hours and expenses, as I've recommended.

Let's say that as a part-time home-based photographer, you put 1,000 hours into your business the first year of operation. Assume further that your overhead expenses amount to $10,000 for the year. Divide the overhead expenses by the hours to arrive at the hourly value or rate—in this case, $10. Some business managers bill the overhead rate separately, as with direct materials and expenses, and enter it as a separate line on the invoice. I don't follow this practice or recommend it. Instead, include it as part of your hourly rate or day rate.

Reducing Costs to Increase Profits

The cost of everything that goes into your business's service or product—materials, supplies, overhead, and labor—affects profit. Your costs must be factored into the fees or prices you charge your clients or customers. Excessive costs can make your fees and prices too high to compete effectively. One result is that you could price yourself out of business.

Consequently, you must remain ever alert for ways to reduce costs and thereby keep your profits up. You must also track your costs to know how to charge them. Cost analysis is a continuing process in any well-run business, and the best tools for this job are your profit-and-loss projections and reports.

If new business operators have a common fault, it's their overly optimistic view of how their businesses will fare. For that reason, it's best to adopt a conservative outlook and tight-fisted management policy.

Don't go into business thinking you'll get rich. Plan, instead, to work hard for an adequate living. If you eventually get rich, good for you. Won't it be a pleasant surprise?

MANAGING ACCOUNTS PAYABLE

Bills that come due regularly are known as accounts payable. There's more to managing this crucial part of your business than simply writing checks and mailing them. You should do so in a timely fashion, and you must understand the difference between *timely* and *on time*.

If you merely stack up all your bills and write checks until you have no more money, you aren't managing well. Although most of your bills are probably payable in thirty days, some vendors offer discounts for payment early in the month—usually something in the range of 1 to 5 percent if paid by the tenth of the month, then net after that. Some vendors make their bills payable in thirty days with no discount option. A typical monthly statement might show "Terms: 2% 10 days—Net 30." That means you have ten days from the date of the statement to deduct 2 percent from your bill; after that, you must pay the full amount, and do so within thirty days of the statement date.

Some suppliers don't send monthly statements but instead expect you to pay off the invoice. You might be allowed a total of thirty days to pay, or until the thirtieth of the month following the invoice date. If the supplier offers an early-payment discount, the invoice might say something like "Terms: 3% 10th proximo—net 30th," which means you may take a 3 percent discount if you pay by the tenth of the month following the invoice date.

Timely Payments

If your checking account is fat, you can just pay all your bills at one sitting, but for most of us, checks and bills arrive throughout the month. Often a checking account balance might make it through only a portion of the bills and need to await the arrival and deposit of the next batch of receivables.

In such circumstances, sort all your bills into stacks, including those offering discounts for early payment, those offering no discounts, and those offering no discounts and charging late-payment penalties. Obviously, the bills to pay first are the discounted ones. I have several vendors who offer 10 percent discounts and one that offers 20 percent; they get paid first every month. Next, pay those that will penalize you for late payment. That way, if you have a slight interruption of cash flow toward the end of the month, you won't have to miss paying a bill that carries a penalty with it.

When the Buck Stops Short

If you continually come up short at the end of the month, you must make some adjustments in your cash-management practices. You should strive to get all your bills paid on time and in a timely way, but when the buck stops short, you need to take action.

Occasionally letting an outstanding balance slip into the thirty-day past-due category is no big deal and will have little or no effect on your credit rating. Balances that go to sixty days are more serious, and ninety days will have your creditors worrying seriously about you.

If you run into a cash-flow problem, the first thing to do is try to inject cash into your business to rectify it. If that's impossible, or if it might cause more serious problems elsewhere, don't just ignore your bills. Immediately write to your creditors to explain the circumstances, assure them that this is a temporary situation that you will correct soon, and provide a date they can count on for full payment.

I ended up in such a position several years ago, after I had placed large orders for office and photographic supplies, counting on a substantial check due from a publisher. The publisher's failure to deliver on time put several of my payables in jeopardy.

I had charged the photographic supplies to a credit card, so I made the minimum payment due and let the balance slip into the high-interest revolving-credit category. The office supplies were charged to my account with the vendor, to whom I wrote a letter and assured full payment within forty-five days. Three weeks later the publisher's check arrived, and I paid my bill and added a 2 percent late charge. Two weeks later I got a letter from the vendor thanking me for the payment; enclosed was a check refunding the late charge.

Such action will leave your credit rating intact, and it might even improve it. Show your business associates that you're a professional and you'll be treated like one.

MANAGING ACCOUNTS RECEIVABLE

Everything owed to you falls into the category of accounts receivable, often just called receivables. Managing receivables is one of the most important aspects of controlling your business's finances.

Get the Cash When You Can

Cash is always best; take it when you can get it. It's impossible, however, to run a photography business without getting involved in credit in one way or another. Whenever you agree to do a job and get paid for it later, you are extending credit. That means credit management is a crucial part of your business.

Billing Practices

Your first step toward managing receivables is to establish systematic billing practices. For most of us, that means stocking and using invoice forms and monthly statement forms. You can pick the forms that best suit your business and have them imprinted with your name, address, and phone number. An alternative is to use a computer to design and generate your own forms. Most word-processing software will facilitate form printing, or you can use any of a number of small-business and form-making programs. Some companies offer multipart, preprinted forms and dedicated software to streamline the billing process.

You must adopt a billing policy and be consistent with it. You can use invoices and monthly statements or invoices alone. In the latter case, ask your clients or customers to pay the invoice and include a statement to that effect on the invoice: *This is the only bill you will receive. Please pay the amount due.*

I use invoices and statements, because the statement often serves as a low-key, impersonal dun on accounts that slip into the thirty-days-past category. So I bill each job with an invoice; then at month's end I send a statement to each customer or client with an outstanding balance. I spell

PHOTO IMAGES UNLIMITED

1492 Columbus Drive ■ Moon Valley, IN 54321 ■ Phone: (123) 555–4545 ■ Fax: (123) 555–6767

INVOICE

Bill to: _____   Ship to: _____

_____   _____

_____   _____

_____   _____

Invoice # _____   Date _____

Customer Order # _____   Terms _____

QUANTITY	ITEM/DESCRIPTION	PRICE	AMOUNT
	TOTAL AMOUNT DUE		

2% per month (24% APR) applied to the balance of all accounts after 30 days

PHOTO IMAGES UNLIMITED

1492 Columbus Drive ■ Moon Valley, IN 54321 ■ Phone: (123) 555–4545 ■ Fax: (123) 555–6767

INVOICE

Bill to: North Coast Country Inn
P.O. Box 1234
Sandra Linda, CA 95432

Ship to: Molly B. Denim, Manager
North Coast Country Inn
1943 Black Sand Beach Dr.
Sandra Linda, CA 95431

Invoice # I-081596-4

Customer Order #

Date August 15, 1996

Terms Net 30 days

QUANTITY	ITEM/DESCRIPTION	PRICE	AMOUNT
1 each	"Wine Country" 16 x 20 print, framed	$250.00	$250.00
1 each	"Redwoods & Rhododendrons" 16 x 20 print, framed	$250.00	$250.00
1 each	"Monarch Elk" 16 x 20 print, framed	$250.00	$250.00
6 each	Assorted Calif. Lighthouse 8 x 10 prints, framed	$125.00	$750.00
6 each	Assorted Calif. Bridge 8 x 10 prints, framed	$125.00	$750.00
2 each	Sunrise/Sunset 11 x 14 prints, framed	$175.00	$350.00
	Total Merchandise		$2,600.00
	Shipping and Handling		50.00
	TOTAL AMOUNT DUE		$2,650.00

2% per month (24% APR) applied to the balance of all accounts after 30 days

PHOTO IMAGES UNLIMITED

1492 Columbus Drive ■ Moon Valley, IN 54321 ■ Phone: (123) 555–4545 ■ Fax: (123) 555–6767

STATEMENT

TO: _____

_____

_____

_____

Date _____

Terms _____

Account Number _____

Amount Past Due _____

DATE	INVOICE NUMBER/DESCRIPTION	CHARGES	CREDITS	BALANCE
	BALANCE FORWARD >>>>>>>			

^ ^ ^ ^ ^ ^ ^
PAY LAST AMOUNT IN THIS COLUMN

2% per month (24% APR) applied to the balance of all accounts after 30 days

PHOTO IMAGES UNLIMITED

1492 Columbus Drive ■ Moon Valley, IN 54321 ■ Phone: (123) 555–4545 ■ Fax: (123) 555–6767

STATEMENT

TO: Accounts Payable Department

North Coast Country Inn

P.O. Box 1234

Sandra Linda, CA 95432

Date	August 31, 1996
Terms	Net 30 days
Account Number	000123
Amount Past Due	

DATE	INVOICE NUMBER/DESCRIPTION	CHARGES	CREDITS	BALANCE
	BALANCE FORWARD >>>>>>>			$1,225.00
8/1/96	Invoice #I-080196-2	$1,875.00		$3,100.00
8/10/96	Payment—Thank You		$1,225.00	$1875.00
8/15/96	Invoice #I-081596-4	$2,650.00		$4,525.00

^ ^ ^ ^ ^ ^ ^

PAY LAST AMOUNT IN THIS COLUMN

2% per month (24% APR) applied to the balance of all accounts after 30 days

out all details of the transaction on the invoice. On the subsequent statement, I need only reference each unpaid invoice by number and show the amount due.

Late Charges and Follow-up

At the bottom of every statement, I rubber-stamp this message in red: *2% per month (24% APR) applied to balance of all accounts after 30 days.* Accounts that go past thirty days get a 2 percent charge added to the balance. After sixty days I also use a bold, red *Past Due* stamp on the statement.

Every account ninety days past due gets the same treatment as the sixty-day account, plus a letter from me insisting on immediate payment. If the account goes to 120 days, I send a demand letter by certified mail, insisting on payment within ten days. The next step is a phone call to my attorney for a ten-day demand letter on his letterhead.

The lawyer's demand letter works nearly every time, but since that one letter will cost me $50, I don't use it for small amounts.

If all those measures fail, I'm faced with the decision to turn the account over to a collection agency or to sue. I have faced such circumstances only twice. In one instance, I decided the likelihood of collection was slim, and the amount wasn't worth the time and trouble, so I wrote it off. In the other case, the amount was worth going after, but even though I was skeptical about the client's promise to pay, I agreed to let her postpone payment for six more months. Three months later her attorney sent me notice of bankruptcy and invited me to stop by to pick up my check for a penny on the dollar, which wouldn't have paid the fuel for the round trip. Live and learn.

PURCHASING

Purchasing is an ongoing process in any business. You will need to spend money on office supplies, photographic supplies and materials, furniture and fixtures, cameras and lenses, and equipment for the office, darkroom, and studio.

It won't take long for you to get a feel for stocking office and photographic supplies and materials and to know what items you need to keep on hand. You'll want to place orders regularly but will probably find monthly to be too frequent. I try to order quarterly, because that keeps paperwork to a minimum and enables me to buy in money-saving quantities. Sometimes I buy more than a three-month supply to take advantage of sales.

Ask for Discounts

Unless you are already buying at rock-bottom prices, don't hesitate to ask your suppliers for better prices, especially local vendors and particularly if you buy in quantity. For example, you shouldn't have to pay a local photo-shop proprietor the same price for film that the casual walk-in does. You represent volume buying and repeat business. If the proprietor doesn't understand this, find another supplier.

Buying Office Supplies

When I started my business, I bought all my office supplies locally, but local vendors' prices eventually drove me out of town. Now I buy all office supplies by mail and save an astounding amount of money each year.

When my printer introduced me to Quill Corporation and gave me one of its catalogs, I started comparing prices and was shocked. A local vendor charged me $3.88 for one fifty-sheet, four-column pad; Quill charged me $8.88 for ten. Color-coded file-folder labels that cost $4.71 a package locally are $1.29 from Quill. Vinyl three-ring binders that range from $4.00 to more than $11.00 here are available from Quill for as little as 89 cents apiece, in quantity. I could buy retail from Quill, add a 200-percent markup, and still sell office supplies for less than the local stationers do. By the way, Quill pays the shipping on all orders over $45, seldom back-orders anything, and delivers to my doorstep in three days or less. (The Quill address is listed at the back of this book, under "Business Equipment and Supplies.")

Buying Photographic Supplies

I buy most of my photography equipment by mail from Norman Camera Company (listed at the back of this book, under "Photographic Equipment and Supplies"), an outfit I've dealt with since the early seventies. Its prices are good, and its services are fast, fair, and reliable. When it's time to upgrade, the company takes trade-ins. It also carries a large inventory and rarely backorders anything.

I can usually beat Norman's film prices by enough to warrant dealing with the outfits that advertise in *Popular Photography* and other magazines, but this has become a terribly tedious and distasteful task. One sleazy trick you'll have to beware of is common to some of these suppliers. You might save considerably on the price of film, mailers, and other materials and equipment, only to get slammed with outrageous shipping and handling charges. Before I knew better, I once ordered a twenty-roll brick of 35mm film and was charged a handling fee of $17, which effectively raised the film price 85 cents a roll.

Despite all the scams and dodges, I still end up getting better prices from these suppliers, but I shop very carefully. When it's time to order, I pore through the ads and list the current prices. I normally stock three kinds of color and two kinds of black-and-white film, so I sometimes have to order from more than one place. I've learned to ask what shipping charges cost, whether the products I'm ordering are in stock, when my order will be shipped, and when any back-ordered items will be delivered.

Purchase Orders

Another form you'll use is the purchase order (PO). Although you won't need POs for local purchases, you will for most mail and phone orders. Printed forms are available at office-supply outlets and by mail from Quill and Nebs (see the Source Directory at the back of this book). You can also use a computer and word-processing software to make your own forms, like the one shown on the following page.

The most obvious advantages of the purchase order are that it provides the vendor with a neat and organized customer order and gives you a record for follow-up. Even if you're ordering by phone, use a PO to keep everything straight and to create a record of the transaction. You needn't fill in all the blanks at the top of the form for phone orders, but at least note the company name and date.

If you've ordered supplies by phone from those big outfits that advertise in the photography magazines, you know that seasons can pass and friends can begin to age noticeably while you sit there on hold. By filling out a purchase order and faxing it to the vendor, you can avoid wasting all that time and still get same-day shipping.

PHOTO IMAGES UNLIMITED

1492 Columbus Drive ▪ Moon Valley, IN 54321 ▪ Phone: (123) 555–4545 ▪ Fax: (123) 555–6767

PURCHASE ORDER

TO: _____

_____

_____

_____

Date _____

Purchase Order # _____

Customer Account _____

Ship Via _____

	QUANTITY	ITEM NUMBER	ITEM DESCRIPTION	PRICE	AMOUNT
1					
2					
3					
4					
5					
6					
7					
8					
9					
10					
11					
12					
13					
14					
15					

Please include one copy of your invoice with the shipment of this order.

PHOTO IMAGES UNLIMITED

1492 Columbus Drive ■ Moon Valley, IN 54321 ■ Phone: (123) 555–4545 ■ Fax: (123) 555–6767

PURCHASE ORDER

TO: Wild Willy's Discount
Photo Supply
77 West 13th Street
New York, NY 10011

Date: August 15, 1996

Purchase Order #: P-081596

Customer Account: *Expires 8/99* 4321 0010 6541 9876

Ship Via: UPS Ground

	QUANTITY	ITEM NUMBER	ITEM DESCRIPTION	PRICE	AMOUNT
1	2 boxes/250		Polycontrast Rapid RCIII F	75.85	$151.70
2	4 each		Dektol for one gallon	3.97	15.88
3	4 each		Rapid Fixer for one gallon	6.95	27.80
4	2 each		T-Max Developer for one gallon	6.99	13.98
5	1 quart		Permawash	6.95	6.95
6	20 each	KR-135-36	Kodachrome 64 Film	5.49	109.80
7	20 each	KL-135-36	Kodachrome 200 Film	6.99	139.80
8	20 each	EB-135-36	Ektachrome Elite 100 Film	6.38	127.60
9	20 each	EL-135-36	Ektacrhome Elite 400 Film	8.59	171.80
10	20 each	TMX-135-36	T-Max 100 Film	3.63	72.60
11	20 each	TMY-135-36	T-Max 400 Film	3.84	76.80
12			TOTAL MERCHANDISE		$914.71
13			SHIPPING, HANDLING, INSUR.		28.04
14			TOTAL ORDER		$942.75
15					

Please include one copy of your invoice with the shipment of this order.

Numbering systems

Preprinted invoice and purchase-order forms come sequentially numbered or unnumbered. If you use unnumbered forms or forms you design yourself, you'll have to devise a numbering system. You can use a simple sequential numbering system, but you'll need to have a way to keep track of the last invoice or purchase order you sent, which can be troublesome. Whatever system you use or invent, make sure you never duplicate a number. In that way, each invoice and purchase order is specific and unique.

Some people prefer a numbering system that employs a six-digit date. It's easy to track, prevents duplication, and is easily modified to fit any situation. To distinguish invoice numbers from purchase-order numbers, prefix the invoice numbers with the letter I and purchase orders with the letter P. If you're sending more than one invoice or purchase order on any day, add a sequentially numbered suffix to each.

Had I used such a system when sending out a batch of invoices on August 16, 1996, here's how it would have worked. The six-digit date was 081696. The first invoice in the batch would have been numbered I-081696-1, the second I-081696-2, and so on. If I had sent but one purchase order that day, its number would have been P-081696.

This system is foolproof and couldn't be simpler.

IS THE LOWEST PRICE ALWAYS THE BEST PRICE?

If you can get the lowest prices and great service, as I do with Quill Corporation, that's the best of both worlds, but it rarely works out that way. You often have to sacrifice one for the other. But when it's a close call, give your business to a local company.

For the first two years I was in business in Oregon, I gave a considerable amount of business to a local photography shop—mostly for darkroom supplies but occasionally for film and smaller pieces of equipment. I never got a nickel off anything I ever bought there, and when I asked the owner about a professional discount, all I got was a vacant stare.

A friend and local high school photography teacher recommended another shop he was dealing with. I no sooner introduced myself to the owner than he offered me a flat 20 percent discount on everything but sale items. His prices are generally higher than those at mail-order suppliers, so I don't buy high-ticket items from him and only occasionally buy film from him. His prices on photographic paper, chemicals, and other darkroom supplies end up being only slightly higher than my mail-order sources.

It wouldn't be any more difficult to buy darkroom supplies by mail, and I would save a little by doing so. Nevertheless, I buy all my darkroom supplies from my local dealer. Let me illustrate my reasoning with a brief example.

I was running down to the wire on an important job and was working through the weekend in order to meet a Monday shipping deadline. I took a thermos of coffee into the darkroom early Sunday morning and set to work. Everything went smoothly until about 9 o'clock, when my enlarger blew a bulb. I always have a backup bulb on hand. Always! Always, except that day.

The photo shop is open Monday through Saturday, and it's the only place in town that carries bulbs for my enlarger. In desperation, I made a phone call, and my friendly dealer cheerfully opened his store to sell me a light bulb. I made my deadline and kept my client happy and coming back for more.

Sometimes the lowest price isn't the best price.

CHAPTER FIVE

THE LEGAL ASPECTS OF YOUR PHOTOGRAPHY BUSINESS

L egal affairs are to the business side of photography what tripods and flash units are to the creative side: necessary nuisances. Although your photography business isn't likely to become entangled in all the legal debris many businesses must contend with, there are legal matters you must consider. The first is to determine whether your business should be a sole proprietorship, partnership, or corporation.

SOLE PROPRIETORSHIP

Most of us who work out of our homes are classified as sole proprietors. That is, we are the only principals involved in the ownership and management of our businesses, and we are the only ones responsible for the outcome. We *solely* reap the benefits, pay the bills, and suffer the consequences of liability.

Even if you have other people working for or with you, you will probably remain the sole proprietor of your business. Having someone else working in your business in no way changes its status. You're not bound to that status forever, so you can always change later. Even if you eventually find partnership or incorporation advantageous, you will probably want to start out as a sole proprietor.

Advantages of Sole Proprietorship

On the plus side is simplicity. There's not much to setting up a sole proprietorship. You aren't encumbered with endless paperwork, and you don't need a lawyer to advise you or create documents for the operation of your business. You pay taxes via your personal return—Schedule C of Form 1040—and your tax rates will usually be lower than corporate rates.

Disadvantages of Sole Proprietorship

Among the disadvantages is difficulty in obtaining outside financing, especially during the start-up stage. You will be entirely responsible for any legal and financial problems your business encounters. You will probably pay much more for health insurance than larger businesses do, and you will be able to deduct only that portion of your premiums allowed on Schedule A (Itemized Deductions) of Form 1040.

PARTNERSHIP

When two or more persons go into business together, they usually form some sort of partnership. Partners share profits, expenses, responsibilities, and liabilities. They might have equal divisions of the business or some other limited arrangement.

Partners enjoy the same tax breaks as sole proprietors. Each reports business profit and loss on Schedule C of Form 1040. It's fairly easy to set up a partnership, and doing so doesn't cost much in the way of attorney's fees.

Advantages of Partnership

Among the advantages of partnership for home-based photographers is the division of major equipment costs. For example, one partner might be responsible for setting up and equipping a darkroom, while the other would see to studio needs. The two then work out agreeable schedules for the use of these facilities.

Sharing costs and use of many high-ticket items makes sense, seeing as such equipment often stands idle much of the time. Photographic partners can share computer hardware and software, expensive copying and duplicating equipment, projection systems, costly lenses, and much more.

The sharing of labor and brain power can lead to the landing of big jobs and contracts the lone photographer might not be equipped to handle. So partnership can lead to many commercial, industrial, and government opportunities.

Disadvantages of Partnership

Partnerships face the same financial difficulties and liabilities as sole proprietorships. Division of management responsibilities can lead to disagreements. And there are always potential problems awaiting the day when a partner leaves the business, for whatever reason.

Those considering partnership must breach numerous obstacles and work out many potential problems. Will the business operate out of one home or both? If one, which one? Will partners carry equal workloads? How will they measure work? Will investments be equal?

Partnership Agreement

Any partnership requires a good written agreement. The better and more complete the agreement, the fewer the hassles down the line. Partners should spend time, individually and together, considering, discussing, and writing down everything pertaining to the business and partnership. Set everything you can think of in writing.

When you decide on an attorney, give that attorney a copy of the document you and your partner or partners have created, and set up a later meeting date. Your attorney should then draft an agreement for approval of all parties. After corrections, additions, and deletions, the attorney will draft the final agreement for partners' signatures.

The agreement should make provisions for division of expenditures, profits, losses, responsibilities, and liabilities, as well as prolonged illness, disability, or death of a partner. You must also consider the disposition of the share of a partner who retires from the business or leaves for any other reason. Include a buy-out clause, and have your attorney advise you on restrictions pertaining to buying and selling of the business or any partner's share. You may want to include nondisclosure and noncompetition clauses.

The agreement can be revised or amended at any time, and it should be whenever the partners make major changes in the way the business is operated. Put it in writing, and keep it current.

Limited-Liability Company

A limited-liability company is a partnership that enjoys some of the advantages usually restricted to corporations. If you're thinking about forming a partnership, ask your attorney about the possibility and advantages of forming a limited-liability company.

CORPORATION

It's highly unlikely that you will want to consider incorporating when you start your business; in fact, you might never want to incorporate. In the event your circumstances change, however, you should know something about the pros and cons. A good attorney and accountant will be able to advise you on this major step.

Incorporation can be expensive. You will certainly need an attorney's help, and you will have to pay your state a fee that might amount to $1,000 or more.

In a sole proprietorship or partnership, the principals are the business, and vice versa; everything that affects the business affects the owners. A corporation is an entity in and of itself.

Advantages of Incorporation

In a corporation, shareholders' assets are protected and corporate assets are initially protected by current bankruptcy laws. Depending on the type of business, corporations generally find financing more readily available than sole proprietorships and partnerships do.

Disadvantages of Incorporation

On the down side, corporations are much more complicated and expensive to set up. Most pay high corporate tax rates. In general, a corporation faces more complications, with requirements for bylaws, a board of directors, corporate officers, annual meetings, and greater need for attorneys and accountants.

ZONING ORDINANCES

Municipalities and counties throughout the nation create urban and rural zones to allow, prohibit, promote, or discourage various activities. Certain areas and neighborhoods might be zoned agricultural, industrial, light industrial, heavy industrial, commercial, residential, and even such combinations as multiresidential or commercial-residential.

In some residential neighborhoods all business is prohibited, no matter what form it takes. Such restrictive zoning, however, is rare.

Obviously, you'll have no problem running your business in any industrial, commercial, or commercial-residential zone. Nor will county officials give you any trouble about operating in an agricultural zone.

Restrictive zoning of most residential neighborhoods is aimed at businesses that create noise, pollution, heavy traffic, and other activities best confined to industrial and commercial zones. Many allow professional and service businesses to operate, so you probably won't have any opposition to your running a home-based photography business. You need to be sure, though, so you'll have to check. Here, again, your local Small Business Development Center should be able to help. You can also check at city hall or your county offices.

NAMING AND LICENSING YOUR BUSINESS

Your business must have a name, but it needn't be any more than your own name. It can be your name or part of your name with or without other elements, or it can be entirely made up, with no reference to your name.

If you have already decided on a business name—your own or an assumed, or fictitious, name—you need only determine what your legal requirements are and how you should go about fulfilling them. If you're undecided, a helpful exercise is one writers and editors use when searching for just the right title. They list the possibilities and examine their merits. Let's take a look at how such a list might shape up for someone named Kim Watson, who's trying to name a home-based photography business. Here are some possible combinations:

1. Kim Watson
2. Kim Watson Photography
3. Kim Watson, Photographer
4. Watson's Photography
5. Watson's Studio
6. Kim Watson's Photo Shop
7. Kim Watson's Photo Images
8. Kim Watson's Photo Factory
9. Photography by Watson
10. Kim's Photo Shop
11. Kim Watson's Portrait Studio
12. Watson and Company
13. Kim Watson and Associates
14. Kim Watson Multimedia Enterprises
15. Photo Images
16. The Photo Factory
17. The Picture Company
18. The Image Factory
19. The Image Emporium
20. Photo Images Unlimited

See how it works? By listing all the names that occur to you and switching elements about, within minutes you will have a working list. In an hour you could probably come up with fifty or more names. Just list as many as appeal to you; then begin eliminating those you like least.

Registering Your Business Name

Before choosing a name for your business, you'll need to learn about any legal restrictions. Depending on state law or local ordinances, you may or may not have to register your business name; even if you're not required to do so, you may want to. Visit your local Small Business Development Center or chamber of commerce, and ask for information about registering a business name.

Where I live, a person who uses what the rule writers call a "real and true name" as a business name need not register the name or pay the filing fee. A real and true name is defined as a person's surname with the given name or initials. My real and true name is Kenn Oberrecht, Kenneth Oberrecht, G. Kenneth Oberrecht, or G. K. Oberrecht.

My state also permits the entrepreneur to add descriptive words to the real and true name without its becoming an assumed business name, which must be registered. If you add certain words that imply additional owners, however—such as *associates*, *company*, or *sons*—you may have to register it as an assumed name, as is the case in my state.

Let's take another look at the list of possible names for Kim Watson's business and assume Kim has moved to Coos County, Oregon, and wants to set up a home-based business there. Put a checkmark by each of the listed names that won't require registration.

Numbers 15 through 20 are obviously assumed names and must be registered. Of the remaining names, numbers 4, 5, 9, 10, 12, and 13 would also require registration.

Even though number 14 would not require registration, it's a terrible business name. It's too long. Shortened to Kim Watson Enterprises, it would still escape registration requirements but would then be too vague.

Mistakes to Avoid

In naming your business, avoid vogue words, slang, and clichés. Don't be too cute. There's nothing wrong with a good catchy name, but a fine line divides catchy business names from cutesy ones.

Stay away from names that are too obscure or esoteric for the general public, or any that are otherwise inappropriate. The F-Stop Shop or The Awesome Aperture might mean something to you but can be meaningless to most of your potential customers. Aardvark Photography will probably get you listed first in the Yellow Pages but might also detour prospective clients who assume you specialize in photographing anteaters.

You want your business name to be remembered. It should be easy to say and easy to spell. If you have a name like mine, I strongly recommend paying the filing fee and adopting an assumed business name.

Don't let your business name limit you. Watson's Portrait Studio meets all the essential criteria for a good business name, but what happens when Kim gets interested in commercial photography or decides to branch out into publication, architectural, or aerial photography? The name becomes obsolete.

Photography is a broad field, and for most home-based businesses, reference to photography in the name should provide the necessary information and diversity. Watson's Photography, Kim's Photo Factory, or F-Stop Photo Shop should work fine for Kim and customers alike.

Licenses and Permits

When you visit the Small Business Development Center or local governmental offices, inquire about any requirements for licenses or permits. You might need some kind of paper issued by the state, county, or city you live in.

In Alaska I had to be licensed by the state. In Oregon there's no such state requirement. In fact, I live in a community consisting of the side-by-side cities of Coos Bay and North Bend. In Coos Bay I would have to have a business license; in North Bend I don't.

There's usually a small annual fee associated with business licenses or permits. Failing to be properly licensed, however, could cost you a stiff fine or even put you out of business.

HIRING AN ATTORNEY

Some people may think lawyers are a necessary evil. I'm not sure if *evil* is the right word, but in today's business climate they are definitely necessary.

Do You Need a Lawyer?

The important question is, Do *you* need a lawyer? Let's hope you never will, but the odds are against that likelihood. Americans are the most litigious people in the world. No wonder; we make up only 5 percent of the world's population, but we have 75 percent of the world's lawyers.

Do you need a lawyer? Probably. Do you need one right now? Probably not, but you should keep one handy. That means you must find a lawyer with a good reputation, make an appointment, and discuss your plans. There should be no charge for this initial meeting, and you should feel no obligation toward the lawyer or law firm. If, for any reason, you're uncomfortable or uneasy with this lawyer, try another. In fact, you might want to meet with several before deciding on which one would be ideal as your legal adviser.

Finding the Right Lawyer

The best way to locate prospective lawyers is to ask around. If you know other photographers and entrepreneurs in your community, ask who their lawyers are and if they're satisfied with the service they're getting.

Your state bar association might have a referral service. Check the Yellow Pages of the phone directory under "Attorneys—Referral," or phone your local Small Business Development Center. There's probably a toll-free number available for the state bar association.

Many lawyers specialize, so you can narrow your choices by eliminating those prospects who work primarily in areas irrelevant to your needs, such as probate, divorce, juvenile, mortgage, immigration, bankruptcy, or personal-injury law. Look, instead, for a lawyer with a general practice and experience in contract and business law. The same lawyer will probably be able to handle your personal legal matters as well. Should the need for a specialist arise—say, for someone versed in copyright law—your attorney will probably be able to refer you to a competent colleague.

INSURING YOUR HOME-BASED BUSINESS

An insurance agent should be more than someone who peddles policies and collects commissions, so you will have to shop around for the right agency and insurance companies. I used the plural *companies* because you will need several policies and might have to deal with more than one company. Independent agents, however, write policies for various companies, so it's possible to work with one agent for all your insurance needs. In any case, you should review your insurance requirements and policies annually and compare prices.

Will Your Homeowner's Policy Suffice?

Your homeowner's or renter's policy may or may not cover your business. That's the first thing to find out. Even if it does, there may be limits to the coverage on some expensive equipment. For example, cameras and lenses might be covered, but only for a few hundred dollars. So you will want to list certain items and get additional coverage for them. You might need a rider on your policy to cover your business as well as your home and all its contents.

Scheduling Equipment for All-Risk Coverage

I travel a good bit and always have with me camera gear worth several thousand dollars. I'm also frequently on the water, boating or canoeing with photographic gear along. I not only have all such equipment listed but also carry replacement-value, all-risk coverage on it. So it's covered on and off my property against theft or loss for any reason.

The list I provided to my insurance agent shows every camera, camera body, lens, motor drive, electronic-flash unit, tripod, exposure meter, and other expensive equipment, with serial number and current replacement value. I also list "filters and lens attachments" as one item and "miscellaneous" as another, each with a replacement value. I have the list on a computer disk, so it's easy for me to send a revision to my agent whenever I buy, sell, or trade in a piece of equipment.

Vehicle Insurance

There was a time when most of us took out a vehicle policy and stayed with the same company permanently. Policies were nearly identical, and rates were similar. Not so now. Rates and coverage can vary considerably from company to company. So look around, and remain alert for better deals.

If you have a good driving record and you get tired of paying high premiums to cover the people who don't, do as I did several years ago: Tell your agent you want a better deal. If he can't offer you lower rates, find a company or agent who will. Be aware, though, that some of these companies will offer attractive rates to get your business, then after a year or so will start increasing your premiums until they're right back where they were. That's when it's time to go shopping again.

People used to look for a company that offered good coverage on a vehicle policy, would not drop a client merely for having a chargeable accident, and would pay claims promptly and adequately. Now many companies will drop you in a blink, and you can count on claims hassles and a fight for every nickel owed you. So if you're going to get stuck with that kind of service, why not pay the lowest possible rates?

Do You Need Extra Liability Insurance?

Liability insurance is expensive, and that included in your homeowner's or renter's policy may not be adequate for your business. If you specialize in portrait photography or any other field that will have customers or clients coming to your property, you'll probably need extra liability coverage, so discuss that with your agent.

Disability and Health Insurance

If you're young and healthy, you should probably consider disability insurance. The older you get, and the more health problems you have, however, the higher the premiums will be. In fact, they quickly rise to prohibitive levels.

Conversely, the younger and healthier you are, the cheaper your health insurance will be. No matter your age or condition, though, as a self-employed person you can count on paying the highest premiums for the poorest coverage. Some professional associations offer group rates for their members, but don't expect any terrific bargains. From the standpoint of health insurance, your best prospect is to be married to a working spouse whose employer offers good coverage.

Life Insurance

Life insurance is a complicated matter about which few generalizations are possible. You must assess your own situation to determine what kind of coverage, if any, you will want or need. If your death and the loss of income from your photography business would create financial hardship for anyone, you probably need some kind of life-insurance policy, either term or whole life. Talk to your agent about it.

Finding an Insurance Agent

Find an insurance agent the way you would find an attorney or accountant. Ask others for recommendations. Talk to several agents, and pick the one who seems to know the most about the insurance business and can assure you of looking out for your best interests. Keep in mind, though, that every insurance agent is first and foremost a salesperson; your best interests are secondary.

COPYRIGHT

Copyright is a form of protection for original works that authors, poets, playwrights, composers, choreographers, artists, photographers, and other creators enjoy. It is afforded more or less automatically to any work, immediately on its creation in fixed form, and the copyright on the work normally becomes the property of the author or creator.

Registering Copyright

Filling out a form and paying the necessary fee to the U.S. Copyright Office does not copyright a work. Copyright is part and parcel of the creation process. If you create a work in fixed form, it is copyrighted and you own the copyright, unless you were an employee of a company and that company paid you to create the work, or you were not an employee but created the work under the terms of a work-for-hire agreement. Filing the paperwork and paying the fee *registers* the copyright.

There is no requirement to register a copyright, but it's best to do so as a way of claiming your copyright. Registration helps immensely if you ever need to sue someone for copyright infringement.

Material That Can Be Copyrighted

Copyright is available for unpublished and published works. It protects all unpublished works. It protects virtually all published works created by United States citizens and most foreign residents in the United States, as well as citizens of foreign nations that are signatories of one of the various copyright treaties to which the United States is also a party.

Among the various kinds of copyright-protected works, those you are most likely to create, use, or come in contact with in your business are literary works, photographs, graphic works, maps, and computer software.

Material That Cannot Be Copyrighted

Some material is not eligible for copyright, such as ideas, procedures, principles, names, titles, slogans, short phrases, lettering, familiar symbols, and typographic ornamentation. Most government-prepared material is also public domain and cannot be copyrighted.

Ownership and Rights

Mere ownership of a work does not grant copyright to or imply copyright by the owner. Unless otherwise agreed upon in writing, copyright belongs to the creator of the work. For example, if you sell someone a matted and framed display print, the person who buys it indeed owns that print and may keep or dispose of it in any way, including selling it for a profit. But that person may not legally copy or reproduce the print in any way without your written consent. You retain the copyright and may produce and sell as many duplicates as you wish unless the print is part of a limited-edition run.

Similarly, when you sell a photograph for publication—in a newspaper, magazine, book, calendar, greeting card, or postcard or in any other medium—you actually sell not the photograph but rather the *right to use* that photograph for a specific purpose. Usually, the right is for one-time use only, unless otherwise specified. You retain ownership of the photograph, copyright, and all residual and subsidiary rights.

Publication with Proper Notice

Before 1978, to be copyrighted most works had to be published with an acceptable copyright notice. Although virtually all works, published or not, are now protected, publication with the proper copyright notice is still important.

The Copyright Office defines publication as "the distribution of copies . . . of a work to the public by sale or other transfer of ownership, or by rental, lease, or lending." Publication photography is not the only area where you need to concern yourself with copyright matters. If you sell salon or display prints through art galleries or at art exhibits and craft shows, you are effectively publishing your work, and it should bear proper copyright notice. Copies of your work appearing as posters, postcards, greeting cards, T-shirt images, and fine-art prints should bear your copyright, as should any of your photographs appearing in any noncopyrighted publication.

As of March 1, 1989, use of the copyright notice became optional;

before then it was mandatory. I recommend you follow the practice, however, because it offers certain distinct advantages. A copyright notice shows the year of first publication, which is an important reference. It identifies you as the owner of the copyright, and it serves notice to the public that the work is protected.

Most important, if the copyright is infringed but the work carried the proper notice, the court will not allow a defendant to claim ignorance. Damages awarded might go as high as $10,000 per infringement and in some cases could be up to $50,000. You may successfully sue for infringement even if the work did not bear copyright notice, but the claim can be deemed "innocent infringement" and result in greatly reduced damages, perhaps as little as $100.

A proper copyright notice has three important elements: (1) the copyright symbol (the letter *c* inside a circle), or the word *Copyright*, or the abbreviation *Copyr.*; (2) the year of first publication; and (3) the copyright owner's name. Example: Copyright 1996 by Kenn Oberrecht.

How Long Does a Copyright Last?

Any work copyrighted on or after January 1, 1978, is protected for a period consisting of the author's or creator's life, plus fifty years. Any work created but not published before January 1, 1978, is now afforded the same protection.

Under the old Copyright Act of 1909, works could be copyrighted for twenty-eight years; then copyright could be renewed for another twenty-eight years, for a total of fifty-six years. For any copyrights in effect on January 1, 1978, the renewal term has been increased to forty-seven years, affording maximum copyright protection of seventy-five years. But such copyrights *must be renewed.*

Once a copyright expires, the work or property becomes public domain and may be freely used by anyone. Prior to January 1, 1978, improper copyright notice or failure to use a copyright notice on first publication often rendered works public domain.

For additional information on copyright, visit your local public library. The Copyright Office will also send you a packet of publications on copyright, as well as the proper forms and instructions for registering copyright (see address at the back of this book, under "U.S. Government.")

CONTRACTS

A contract is an enforceable agreement between or among two or more parties, permitting or prohibiting certain actions and activities, with mutual but not always equal benefits accruing to each party. Contracts of some form or another are used in most businesses.

Professional photographers use various kinds of contracts in their work: publishing agreements, agency agreements, transfer-of-rights agreements, work-for-hire agreements, model releases, and work orders, among others. You might use any or all of these, depending on the nature of your work.

Transfer-of-Rights and Work-for-Hire Agreements

If you work as a publication photographer, you will be required to sign contracts usually generated by the publishers. These are commonly transfer-of-rights agreements that specify the rights you are granting. Some publishers, whose interpretation of the letter and intent of the copyright statutes is extremely broad, use work-for-hire agreements instead. These effectively force you to give up all rights in and ownership of the work.

Some publishers' transfer-of-rights agreements stipulate that the purchase is for all rights or world rights, which, of course, leaves the photographer without any future rights to use the work. I suggest you adopt the policy of selling only one-time publication rights to any photograph. If a publisher insists on buying all rights or using a work-for-hire agreement, either decline or insist on much higher payment than you might get for one-time use.

Keep in mind that a single transparency or negative might generate numerous sales for years to come. Many professional photographers have photographs on file that have sold over and over again and earned thousands of dollars. You relinquish that potential whenever you agree to sell all rights to a photograph or sign a work-for-hire agreement.

Don't be intimidated by all the legalese contained in a transfer-of-rights agreement that calls for all rights, and don't get into an argument about it with the publisher. The first thing to do with such an agreement is to use a ruler and pen to line out anything in the contract that you don't agree with. Then type or neatly print any of your own stipulations. Sign and date the agreement, initial any changes you have made, and return the form to the publisher.

I've rarely met any opposition to my handling contracts in this way. Publishers and most other clients will try to get as much as they can from you and give as little as possible in return. If you just accept what they try to dictate, you have no one to blame but yourself. You must stand up for your rights and demand fair payment for your work.

Agency Agreements

If you plan to work with a stock agency, you will be asked to sign an agency agreement, which stipulates that for each sale the agency makes, you and the agency split the payment received, usually fifty-fifty, but sometimes better, such as sixty-forty, photographer's favor.

Get Help

If you aren't accustomed to working with contracts and you find their language baffling and full of obfuscation, note the confusing and confounding clauses. Then take the contract and your notes to your attorney for a translation. Pay close attention to what your attorney tells you, and soon you will learn to comprehend contracts without having to pay someone to interpret them for you.

Model Releases

Another common contract photographers use is the model release. A model release is a short and simple agreement between photographer and model, in which the model signs over the rights to the photographer to use the model's photographic image free of encumbrances.

Model releases are required for all photographs with recognizable images of people when used in advertising, sales brochures, catalogs, and many company-sponsored magazines and other publications. Although model releases aren't generally required for photographs used editorially or to illustrate text or editorial copy in books and periodicals, some publishers require them. Moreover, it's a good idea to develop the habit of using them, not only to protect yourself from any potential lawsuit but also to make your photographs as widely salable as possible.

A photographer friend of mine on a Montana ski trip spent a good bit of his weekend shooting photos for calendars, magazines, and other

KIM WATSON, PHOTOGRAPHER

1492 Columbus Drive · Moon Valley, IN 54321 · (123) 555-4545

MODEL RELEASE

DATE: _____   FILE REF: _____

For valuable consideration received, which I hereby acknowledge, I irrevocably grant Kim Watson, and anyone Kim Watson authorizes, the absolute permission to use, reproduce, sell, and resell any pictures of me, or any in which I may appear, in whole or in part, taken this day, and to be used for publishing, advertising, art, trade, or any other lawful purpose.

I hereby waive any right to inspect or approve these pictures or any captions or text that may be used in connection with them, or to approve the use to which such material may be applied.

I hereby release Kim Watson and any of Kim Watson's heirs, executors, administrators, associates, and assigns from liability for any blurring, distortion, alteration, or optical illusion, whether intentional or not, that may result from the making of these pictures.

I am 18 or older: YES _____   NO _____ (Under 18, see section below)

Model's Name (print) _____ Phone _____

Address _____

City _____ State _____ Zip _____

Model (sign) _____

Witness (sign) _____

FOR ANY MODEL UNDER 18 YEARS OF AGE

I hereby certify that I am the parent or legal guardian of the above-named model, and I consent, without reservations, to all the foregoing on behalf of the model.

Parent/Guardian (sign) _____

Witness (sign) _____

Date _____

markets. A magazine bought one-time rights to one of his photographs of three beautiful young women, colorfully clad in ski outfits. Soon after the photograph ran, a ski manufacturer phoned to buy rights to the photograph for many times what the magazine had paid. It turned out that the manufacturer's name clearly appeared on all the skis in the picture. My friend, however, had failed to get his models to sign releases, so there was no sale. You can bet he hasn't made that mistake again.

You needn't worry about model releases for photographs in which people are unrecognizable. If a person is clearly recognizable, however, get a release. Of course, if you're hiring a model for a shoot, a model release should be part of the working contract. When you travel, carry a supply of model releases with you, and use them. You'll find that most people will be thrilled that you want to use their images for publication, and they'll gladly sign your releases.

In contract language, *valuable consideration* simply means money. When you hire a professional model, you will agree on payment before the shoot. When you ask nonprofessionals to sign model releases, most will do it for free. It's a good idea, though, to make sure some small amount of money changes hands. For such purposes I carry a supply of dollar bills and hand one to each model who signs. Even when models wave off my meager offering, which most do, I smile and explain that it just makes the deal binding. That's precisely what it does.

I've seen a number of model releases that just go on and on with all the legal mumbo jumbo imaginable. That might be all right for use with models you hire for jobs, but if you're asking nonprofessionals to pose for you or to sign releases for frames they've shown up in, your model release ought to be as short and simple as possible. You can't ask people for favors and then expect them to sign intimidating documents.

Other Contracts

Some photographers use work orders or job orders to set up contracts with their customers. These are simple forms that you fill in with all the pertinent information and customer's stipulations. It should be imprinted with your conditions and stipulations. When the customer signs the order and receives a copy of it, you and the customer then have a contract for a specific job.

You can have a local printer print work orders and other contract forms, make your own forms, or order them by mail. NEBS, Inc., has a number of such forms available for photographers that the company will imprint with your name, address, and phone number. (The NEBS address is listed at the back of this book, under "Business Equipment and Supplies.") Among NEBS's offerings are a wedding-photography contract, a video contract, and a general-photography contract that covers most jobs. The company will also custom-print contract forms for you.

CHAPTER SIX

WRITING A BUSINESS PLAN

A business plan is your blueprint for success. It's not something you devise and abandon once you're in business. It's a working, changing, growing document, the basis for all your future forecasting and goal setting. If you want your home-based business to succeed, you must plan for its success.

A business plan is a detailed scheme describing how a proposed or existing proprietorship, partnership, or corporation conducts its operations. It's a strategy you work out in advance, designed to define the ways you will finance, operate, and profit from this service-oriented business.

Your business plan can also be a document to use for attracting financial backing or selling your services to potential clients. Moreover, it can help you establish credit and credibility.

I had been operating my business full-time for five years when my wife and I decided to build the house we now occupy. My financial planning and forecasting helped me to prepare a convincing document that ultimately led to qualification for a home mortgage with a very attractive interest rate. It enabled me to expand my business from a small office and jury-rigged darkroom to a comfortable, cedar-paneled office, large studio, complete darkroom, and shop.

Drafting a business plan requires careful thought, effort, and time. Don't try dashing it off over a weekend. Take the task seriously, and give it the time it needs.

I must confess that when I started my business, I did not have a written business plan. I had a good idea of what I wanted to do and how I intended to accomplish it. Over the years, I had also given a lot of thought to the business. I had studied, spent years in college, and researched the areas my college courses hadn't covered.

I'm not sure a written plan would have made a great difference in the early, part-time years of my business. Nevertheless, I'm convinced that a formal plan would have forced me to consider aspects of the business I had ignored and would have alerted me to potential problems I could have averted.

For most prospective entrepreneurs, the toughest part of writing a business plan is getting started. If you've read the first five chapters of this book and followed the directions there, you have already begun putting your plans and ideas on paper, and you should realize by now that it's not such a difficult process.

Writing a business plan is a challenge, but it can be an enjoyable and enlightening exercise that hones your problem-solving skills and provides a foundation to build your business on.

WHY YOU SHOULD WRITE A BUSINESS PLAN

Of the various reasons for writing a business plan, not all apply to the home-based photographer. During the early stages of your operation—perhaps for the life of your business—you needn't worry about mergers, acquisitions, attracting highly skilled employees, or setting up strategic alliances with major corporations.

Your reasons for developing a good plan are more fundamental and pragmatic. Your plan should enable you to do the following:

- *Assess the feasibility of the venture*. You will eventually have to convince others that your home-based photography business is or will be a healthy, viable operation. The first person you must convince, though, is you. A good business plan is the most persuasive tool at your disposal for that purpose. In the final analysis, you'll be able to determine whether you should start your own business or keep your day job.

- *Evaluate business resources*. Listing all your physical assets and professional attributes allows you to determine where your needs lie and what your strengths and weaknesses are. This can serve to reassure you and others and to steer you down the right road.

- *Evaluate financial resources.* Before going into business, you must know what your financial status is and where you'll acquire needed operating capital. You should also have something to fall back on in case of an emergency or something to count on in the event of an investment opportunity.

- *Identify potential clients.* You must know who your clients or customers will be in order to effectively market your services and products to them. You need to identify your immediate buyers and target your future buyers.

- *Establish a workable timetable.* Once you have determined that your venture is feasible and have evaluated your resources and markets, all that's left is to decide when to open your business. You should also make some flexible decisions about growth and progress by plugging future plans into your timetable.

- *Set reasonable and competitive fees or prices.* How will you bill your clients or charge your customers? What do other local photographers charge? You'll need to thoroughly research fee and price structure to ascertain what your services and products are worth and include that information in your business plan.

- *Provide a framework for scheduling.* Time study and scheduling are crucial to business success. You must know not only what any given project or product will cost you to produce but also how much time it will take. Both short-range and long-range scheduling will continue as an integral, ongoing process for the life of your business.

- *Create a basis for forecasting.* Related to the scheduling process is a form of guessing known as forecasting. To forecast business trends, cash flow, and profit margins requires intelligence, experience, a thorough understanding of the competition, a firm grasp of markets, and a top-quality crystal ball. In the absence of the last mentioned, a good business plan is a reasonable substitution.

- *Facilitate the setting of realistic goals.* A business without goals is a trip without a destination—a time-consuming, money-wasting, aimless wandering. It's important to set goals from the start and, as you realize them, to set new ones. Your goals shouldn't be too easily attained or impossible to achieve. They must be on the tough side of realistic.

- *Land important and lucrative jobs.* If you have an opportunity to bid on a corporate or government job, the people letting the contract will want to know all about you and your business. You'll look like a bush-league player if you don't have a confidential business plan ready for limited distribution.

- *Secure bank or investor financing.* Although it's best to avoid borrowing money to run your business—especially during the formative years—you might experience a temporary cash-flow interruption or might need to buy some expensive equipment in order to land a job. A business plan can go a long way toward securing needed funds.

ORGANIZING YOUR BUSINESS PLAN

No rules or formulas exist for preparing a business plan. Just as no two businesses are entirely alike, no two plans can be identical. Business plans vary greatly, even within the same industry.

Eastman Kodak and I are both in the photography business, but I daresay no one will be surprised to learn that our businesses are radically different on every level. My business even differs greatly from other photography businesses in my community.

There's no set length or established format for a business plan. It can be as detailed or abbreviated as you want to make it. Business plans for major companies might run to forty pages or more. I've heard of some reaching a hundred pages. Yours will certainly be shorter—probably something between ten and twenty pages. But don't consider this absolute. Make it whatever length you're comfortable with.

As you begin listing information for your plan, include as many details as you can. Make the rough draft as long as it needs to be without padding. Then work it down to as precise and concise a document as possible.

Remember, a business plan is a working document that is about your operations; it should change as your business does. Consequently, this is not something that simply amounts to filling in the blanks on a form.

Business-plan forms are indeed available from several sources. You'll find them in books on business and publications from the Small Business

Administration, as well as in handouts from a local Small Business Development Center. There are even computer-software programs available. All of these—including this chapter—are only guidelines, designed to help you *write your own business plan.*

Every business plan should be neatly typed or printed on good-quality bond paper, with 1-inch margins on the top, bottom, left, and right. It should have a cover page and table of contents. It's also a good idea to include an executive summary. Other important sections address such topics as organization, finances, management, and marketing. If you wish to include such ancillary documents as a résumé or brief autobiographical statement, credit references, and letters of recommendation, put them in an appendix at the end of the plan.

The plan should be divided into sections, with each section titled according to contents: Executive Summary, The Organizational Plan, The Financial Plan, and so on. Divide the sections with subheads.

Make sure everything about your business plan is as perfect and readable as you can make it. Misspelled words, misplaced punctuation, shabby sentence and paragraph structure, and errors in grammar and syntax leave a mighty poor impression. The implication is, if your business plan is sloppy, maybe your business practices are too.

If you're among the legions who have trouble handling the mechanics of American English, hire help. Find someone who can read your finished plan, locate the errors, and correct them. You'll need a consultant with above-average skills. Keep in mind, though, that just because someone teaches high school or college English or works as a writer or editor doesn't necessarily mean that person is an expert in style, usage, and the mechanics of contemporary American English. In fact, finding such a person may well prove the most difficult part of creating your business plan.

Don't try to impress people with big or fancy words or with how much you happen to know about business or photography. Avoid jargon, clichés, and buzzwords. Keep the language clear, simple, and straightforward.

Even if you are a skilled writer who doesn't need outside help, have someone read your plan and look for those elusive typographical errors and the little obscurities that make a sentence or paragraph cumbersome or awkward. Your plan should be pleasantly readable.

COVER PAGE

Center the phrase *Confidential Business Plan* at the top and bottom of the cover page, preferably in large boldface type. This is a message to anyone who reads or refers to your plan that the contents are not for general distribution.

About a third of the way down the page, center your business name, street address, P.O. box if you have one, phone number, and fax number if you have a dedicated fax line.

Then number each copy you distribute, for whatever reason. Keep a log in your business-plan file that lists every person who receives a copy of your plan, the number on that copy, and the date of distribution. This is another important message to anyone in possession of your business plan. It lets people know that you are keeping tight control of this document and implies that the recipient has the responsibility to safeguard its contents.

TABLE OF CONTENTS

Provide a table of contents as a convenience to the reader. Simply list the various sections of your plan and their corresponding page numbers.

EXECUTIVE SUMMARY

Like the table of contents, the executive summary is provided as a convenience for the reader. Your business plan covers all aspects of your business in detail. The executive summary covers the same subjects but in brief form. Try to distill the essence of your business into one page, with perhaps a paragraph each devoted to the major sections of your business plan.

The executive summary is a courtesy to anyone who will be reading or referring to your business plan for whatever reason. In the minute or so it takes to read this one-page abstract, the reader can determine whether or not to read on or study the plan more closely. That makes this an extremely important part of the business plan.

Like the lead to a magazine article or news story, the executive summary must be as interesting, informative, and relevant as you can make it.

CONFIDENTIAL BUSINESS PLAN

Photo Images Unlimited
1492 Columbus Drive
Moon Valley, IN 54321

Phone: (123) 555–4545
Fax: (123) 555–6767

Proprietor: Kim Watson

Copy Number _____

CONFIDENTIAL BUSINESS PLAN

THE ORGANIZATIONAL PLAN

Here's where you lay out the specifics of your business organization. Start by identifying yourself and your business as a sole proprietorship, partnership, or corporation. Your home-based photography business will doubtless begin as a sole proprietorship, and chances are, it will remain in that status.

If you have one or more persons working with or for you, include that information. Tell whether these are full-time, part-time, permanent, or temporary employees or associates. Discuss their contributions to the operation of your business. If they're family members, mention that too.

You need to indicate why your business exists and how it functions. Discuss its strengths, your business philosophies, and your photographic skills. Resist any temptation to get technical.

Provide a clear picture of where you stand as you plan to launch your business and where you *intend* (don't use the word *hope*) to be a year from now, two years from now, and five years out. Demonstrate that you have immediate objectives and long-range goals. Write about the scope and direction of your business, and tell what your scheduled operating hours and days are.

THE FINANCIAL PLAN

This is the most important part of your business plan. That's why two chapters in this book are devoted to financial planning and management. If you have read Chapters 3 and 4 and prepared the financial documents covered there, you have already done most of the work required for this section of the business plan.

Statement of Financial Condition

Begin the section with a brief narrative statement of your financial situation, followed by a statement of financial condition, also known as a personal financial statement or statement of net worth. (See the section in Chapter 3 on "The Personal Financial Statement.")

For the beginning entrepreneur, this is the only part of the financial plan that can be precise. The rest of it is an educated guess at best, but you'll be called on to make such guesses more often than you might think, especially by lending institutions, the Internal Revenue Service, and perhaps your state revenue agency.

Sources of Funds

Here is where you divulge your financial sources. The old saw, "It takes money to make money," applies to every business. You can't expect to attract clients or customers if you haven't carefully and wisely invested in assets and made plans to capitalize your business. What's more, investment and capitalization are continuing processes, lasting as long as you remain in business.

The chief function of a business plan is to provide an accurate appraisal of your business's financial health. This is not just so you can secure loans or entice financial backers; it should also make financial management easier for you.

Include a short report in your business plan called "Sources of Funds," which should list your assets, their worth, and their sources, as shown in the accompanying sample.

The "Capital Assets Inventory" form is handy for compiling the figures you'll need. Use a separate form for each type of property listed: furniture and fixtures, office equipment, darkroom equipment, studio equipment, and photography equipment. You need not include these forms in your business plan, because you'll summarize their contents under "Sources of Funds."

The completed inventory forms, stored with your insurance policies, are valuable documents should you ever experience a casualty loss, so it's important to update them regularly. If you carry all-risk coverage for your photography equipment, be sure to send a copy of the appropriate form to your insurance agent each time you update it.

Profit-and-Loss Projection

For purposes of your business plan, prepare a profit-and-loss projection for the upcoming year on a monthly basis, then quarterly for the second year, and annually for the third, fourth, and fifth years. (See details in Chapter 3, "Financial Planning.")

If you are starting your business in midyear, project the remaining months of that year on a monthly basis. So if you start your business in

SOURCES OF FUNDS		
ASSETS	**AMOUNT/COST**	**SOURCES**
Cash	$3,000	Business Savings
Investments	$15,000	Certificates of Deposit
Accounts Receivable	$2,000	Business Sales
Materials and Supplies	$1,500	Currently on Hand
Vehicle	$14,000/$17,500	Installment Purchase
Furniture and Fixtures	$1,300	Currently Owned
Office Equipment	$2,200	Currently Owned
Darkroom Equipment	$800	Currently Owned
Studio Equipment	$400	Currently Owned
Photography Equipment	$3,600	Currently Owned

October, for example, you would project profit and loss on a monthly basis for the first five quarters or fifteen months, then quarterly and annually as described above.

Remember, a business plan is a living, working, evolving document. It should be a five-year plan that you review and modify as necessary—at least once a year.

Balance Sheet

People accustomed to working with balance sheets will no doubt want to see one in your business plan. Prepare one according to directions in Chapter 3.

Cash-Flow Projection

A cash-flow projection will probably prove to be one of your more useful financial documents, so you should include one as part of your business plan. (See details in Chapter 3.) You might also want to discuss how you

CAPITAL ASSETS INVENTORY

Type of property _____   Date of Inventory _____

DESCRIPTION	SERIAL NUMBER	DATE ACQUIRED	COST OR VALUE
TOTAL VALUE			

CAPITAL ASSETS INVENTORY

Type of property _Photography Equipment_   Date of Inventory _August 1, 1996_

DESCRIPTION	SERIAL NUMBER	DATE ACQUIRED	COST OR VALUE
Nikon FM2 Black Body	3136759	1996	$600
Nikon FM2 Black Body	2131108	1990	$500
Nikon 28mm f/2.8 Lens	2864701	1992	$350
Nikon 35-70mm f/3.3 Zoom Lens	2302506	1990	$200
Nikon 100-300mm f/4.5-5.6 Zoom Lens	2229816	1994	$500
Nikon 55mm f/3.5 Macro Lens	357990	1991	$200
Sigma 500mm f/7.2 APO Lens	1002005	1995	$550
Tamrac 610 Pro Bag		1996	$110
Tamrac Convertible Backpack		1995	$120
Tamrac Photographer's Daypack		1996	$ 80
Slik U212 Tripod		1990	$ 90
Filters, Flashes, and Accessories			$300
		TOTAL VALUE	$3,600

use profit-and-loss and cash-flow projections to manage the financial aspects of your business.

THE MANAGEMENT PLAN

In this section you must demonstrate your ability to manage your operation. Various business publications stress the importance of the team concept of management. They insist you list the members of your management team and devote a half-page each to a description of each member's strengths and management experience.

How Many Ponies in Your Show?

If you have other key people in your organization, by all means tell about them. In your home-based photography business, however, you probably represent the entire management staff and labor force.

There's nothing wrong with the one-pony show, provided the star attraction isn't just a one-trick pony. So here's where you will need to describe your show and all the tricks you know. You'll need to discuss your experience and diverse skills. Talk up your abilities and tell how your business will profit from them. I'm not suggesting you embellish the facts; merely uncover them and use them to your best advantage.

Discuss Your Skills and Experience

In courses I've taught, I have worked with students who think they have no valuable experience to lean on, nothing worthwhile to offer. A brief one-on-one conference or interview, however, invariably turns up hidden talents and attributes.

To help you prepare a brief narrative statement, refer to your résumé, or make a list of the jobs you've held and duties you were responsible for. Be relevant. Zero in on jobs and duties that demonstrate management skills.

For instance, if when you were a high-school or college student the state highway department hired you in the summer to pick up roadside litter, that's not relevant. On the other hand, if you were put in charge of a crew of summer workers picking up litter, that shows you have supervisory experience and indicates you can handle responsibility.

If you have photography experience, describe that too. Include amateur as well as professional work. Tell about any awards, exhibits, or special recognition you've had.

You should even include any relevant volunteer or pro bono work and organizational offices you've held. All of this contributes to your business and personal identity and defines who and what you are.

List Your Business Associates

Even if you are the sole proprietor of a one-person operation, you have or should have professional or business associates you should list in your business plan. Provide the name, address, and phone number of your insurance agent, banker, accountant, and lawyer, as well as any photo labs you work with.

Deal Intelligently with Your Weaknesses

Of course, you'll want to elaborate on your strengths as a manager and photographer, but you should also identify your weaknesses and describe the actions you'll take to eliminate them.

For example, if you plan to use a computer in your business and you've had plenty of computer experience, that's a strength worth discussing. If you have had no computer experience, perhaps you plan to take a course or two at a local computer center or community college. Maybe you have a plan to learn on your own with books, videocassettes, and tutorial software.

Weaknesses and insufficiencies are nothing to be ashamed of but if you ignore them or fail to plan for their elimination, they remain an impediment to progress and success. Merely planning sensibly to shore up a weakness can neutralize its effect for the time being. Taking action as planned can turn a weakness into a strength.

THE MARKETING PLAN

The first step in drafting a marketing plan is determining what, exactly, your business will provide to its clientele in the way of products or services. You have probably already determined that. If not, you must do so now.

Identify Your Competition

Deciding on what your photography business will sell helps establish your niche in the marketplace. Knowing this makes it easy to identify your competition and how you will deal with it.

Identify Your Markets

Developing a sound marketing plan requires market analysis. You need to conduct some methodical but fairly simple research to determine who your potential customers are and how many are out there.

If you intend to shoot school portraits, you need only determine how many students there are in your vicinity to arrive at a base figure. You may want to narrow your approach to include only high-school students, or maybe graduating seniors only. A few phone calls will provide you with the numbers you need.

If you're a wedding photographer, every couple who gets married in your community represents a potential job. Someone at your local daily newspaper should be able to tell you roughly how many wedding announcements run every week, month, or year, to provide you with a base number.

Likewise for the photographer interested in commercial, industrial, real estate, architectural, legal, or medical photography. A trip through the Yellow Pages of the phone directory or some time spent with a locally published city or business directory should provide the numbers you need.

If your chief area of expertise or interest is publication photography, most of your markets will probably be outside your community. Nevertheless, you shouldn't overlook local daily and weekly newspapers, Sunday or weekend supplements, city and regional magazines, local book publishers and advertising agencies, and any local company that produces house organs or employee publications. Add to this the stock agencies and national publishers of books, trade magazines, and popular periodicals, as well as publishers of calendars, posters, greeting cards, and postcards, and you will soon arrive at an impressive number of potential clients.

Determine Your Market Share

Determining your market share is a bit more difficult, but since it mainly requires guesswork, your figures aren't easily challenged. Be realistic and conservative in your estimates, and you'll probably outperform your best guess.

You might discover that you don't have the capacity to take full advantage of your market share. For example, let's say there are about 500 weddings a year in your city. If you work alone, and you hustle enough to manage one wedding a week, that would be a 10 percent share of the market. As your name and work get known, you may well find that you have more business than you can handle, at which time you will no doubt want to consider expansion or collaboration.

Your marketing plan boils down to a fair assessment of the marketplace, how you will compete, who your potential customers are, what your market share amounts to, and how you will deal with growing demands on your business. After seeing to the necessary research and market analysis, put all this into narrative form and include it in your business plan.

APPENDICES

You may or may not wish to include appendices. If you have sterling credentials, though, you should seriously consider putting them into your business plan.

This is the place to include your résumé, a list of where you have published or exhibited photographs, a list of business and personal references, a list of credit references, and copies of letters of recommendation or commendation.

CHAPTER SEVEN

TAXES AND RECORD KEEPING

These days, it seems tax collectors are coming at us from every direction. Depending on where you live and do business, you might have to pay city, state, and federal income taxes; self-employment tax; personal property and real-estate taxes; city, borough, county, or state sales tax; state and federal fuel taxes; room tax; and an assortment of other taxes disguised as user fees, license fees, application fees, registration fees, permit fees, and filing fees.

You will need to determine the kinds of taxes you must pay in your city, county, and state. If you don't already know, check with your local Small Business Development Center, the chamber of commerce, or the local office of your state revenue department.

All of us must pay federal taxes, which we'll discuss momentarily. Because circumstances vary, even among people who are in the same business, and because tax codes and their numerous supporting documents exist in a constant state of change, it's impossible to provide specific advice. Furthermore, in the space of a chapter, I can provide only an introduction to taxes and taxation. I'll try to pass on some helpful tips and give you a good enough grounding in the concepts so you will be able to continue on your own.

In dealing with your taxes and essential record keeping, you can be involved at any level you wish, ranging from doing it all yourself to hiring others to do most of it for you. In any case, you need to understand what your responsibilities are. Even if you decide to turn everything over to someone else, you will still have to see to some tax chores.

Your options are several. You can do your own bookkeeping or can hire a bookkeeper. You can prepare your own tax returns and associated forms and schedules or can have a professional tax preparer, accountant, or attorney do it for you. The choices are yours, but I am going to make some recommendations.

First, keeping books is relatively easy, so I suggest you do it yourself, especially the first year or so you're in business. This not only will help you contain start-up costs but also will introduce you to the fundamentals of record keeping.

I continue to do my own bookkeeping after all these years because it helps me stay in touch with the financial aspects of my business and lets me know how I'm doing from month to month. What's more, a book-keeper would be one more person I'd have to deal with in my busy life, and I'd rather not just now. Besides, by the time I've collected and sorted all my receipts, bills, canceled checks, and such, all that remains is entering the information on ledger pages and running the numbers through my calculator (or entering the information on a computer screen and letting the program do the rest). It's no big deal.

I'm not about to tell you that doing your own taxes is easy. Far from it. It's a tedious, often confusing, sometimes infuriating task. Never-theless, I recommend you try your hand at it as a way of learning about taxation and how it affects your business. Once you've had the experience, decide for yourself whether to continue on your own or hire help. Learning how to keep books and prepare your tax returns enables you to provide better, more complete information when you decide to turn it all over to someone else.

You might want to try one of the computer-software packages designed for preparing tax returns, but a few caveats are in order first. These programs vary greatly in quality, you'll have to buy new software every year, and you might not like the results.

NBC's *Today* show ran a review of several such programs, all of which led the user to make expensive tax overpayments. The reviewer recom-mended buying and using one of the programs as a way of keeping tidy records but then hiring an aggressive accountant to review tax returns and the various computer-generated forms. My advice is to shop careful-ly and ask colleagues and business acquaintances for recommendations before buying this or any other kind of software.

The tendency of most Americans is to put off the tax chores as long as possible. Don't join the herd, especially if you decide to try preparing your own returns. You probably won't have all the documents you need until the end of January, so spend that month gathering all your essential forms, schedules, publications, and antacid tablets. Plan to work on your returns in February. That way, if you find you need help or discover that you don't have all the necessary documents, you'll have time and won't need to panic, or worse, pay a penalty for filing late.

USING YOUR HOME FOR YOUR BUSINESS

As a home-based photographer, you should be able to take a tax deduction for any rooms you use *exclusively* and *regularly* for conducting your business. This can include an office, studio, darkroom, storage room, waiting room, shop, gallery, or combinations thereof. A studio, for example, need not be used exclusively as a studio, but it must be used exclusively as part of your business. My studio is a multipurpose room that houses my studio lights, seamless backgrounds, setup table, and copy stand, but it also has a desk and worktable where I do sorting, mounting, matting, and some framing. Much of my reference library is on the bookshelves that line two walls of my studio. Along another wall are filing cabinets. So this room functions as a studio, library, and storage area, while serving other business purposes as well.

If you plan to use only a portion of the space in a garage, basement, attic, or other large open area for business use, you might consider partitioning it to take advantage of allowable tax deductions. For example, you could partition off a room to use exclusively as an office or office-studio combination, thereby enabling you to take a business deduction for the square footage of that room, even though the remaining area may be used for personal or household purposes.

Another possibility would be to convert a spare room into a home office and partition off one corner of a basement or garage where plumbing is available to set up a darkroom. You could then take a deduction for the square footage of your office and darkroom.

Similarly, you can take a deduction for a room you use for storage. You cannot simply put up shelves or cabinets for business storage in a room you use for other personal or household purposes, then take a deduction for that space. You can, however, partition off that space to create a separate room, thus making that square footage eligible for the deduction.

What Is a Home?

House and *home* are not synonyms. A house is a building in which people live. A home is any dwelling that provides shelter for people or functions as a residence or multiple residence. You don't have to live in a house in order to qualify for deductions for the business use of your home. The Internal Revenue Service (IRS) uses the broader term *home* to mean "house, apartment, condominium, mobile home, or boat." The IRS's definition also includes "structures on the property, such as an unattached garage, studio, barn, or greenhouse."

USE TEST

You may be entitled to limited deductions for the business use of your home, but such use must meet certain criteria.

Exclusive Use

That portion of your home used for business purposes must be used exclusively for such purposes in order to qualify for a tax deduction. You can't use a room as a studio, sewing room, and guest quarters, then claim a business deduction for it or any portion of it.

Regular Use

You must regularly use this part of your home for business, but this stipulation has more to do with continuity than frequency. For example, if you mostly shoot color and send it out for processing, you can't justify taking a deduction for a darkroom you might use once or twice a year for clients who want black-and-white photographs, even if you use the room for no other purpose. If you regularly spend a day a week, or even only a day a month, working in your darkroom, that should constitute regular use on a continuing basis and should help qualify the room for the deduction.

Principal Place of Business

Here's a source of potential confusion. If you are a full-time home-based photographer, your home should qualify as your principal place of business, and the space you have set up for doing business should be eligible for a limited deduction. If you have a photography shop and studio downtown, however, and decide to set up an office at home for seeing to various business tasks, your home office probably would not be eligible under the current regulations, because it is not your principal place of business.

Interestingly, though, the IRS recognizes the fact that you can have more than one principal place of business, provided you're engaged in more than one business. For instance, if you teach photography full-time at a local community college and work weekends out of your home as a wedding photographer, you could have two principal places of business: the college, where you are in the full-time teaching business, and your home, where you are in the part-time photography business. So you should be able to take the home-office deduction, so long as you meet the other criteria. Or you could be a lab technician, motorcycle mechanic, chef, plumber, cop, or computer programmer five days a week and run a part-time photography business from your home and still qualify for the deduction.

Separate Structures

The IRS also allows deductions for separate freestanding structures, such as a detached garage, barn, studio, shop, or storage building, providing it's used exclusively and regularly for business. If you have any such structures on your property, they might suit your purposes. Keep in mind, too, that as your business matures, it might outgrow its space. Separate structures could prove the ideal solution to that problem.

Trade or Business Use

According to the IRS, "You must use your home in connection with a trade or business to take a deduction for its business use." Your home-based photography business should easily meet this criterion.

Calculating Your Business Percentage

The allowable deduction for operating a business from your home is based on the percentage of total home space your business occupies. It's a simple matter of arithmetic accomplished in three easy steps:

1. Determine the square footage of your entire home.
2. Determine the square footage of your business space.
3. Divide the square footage of your business space by the total square footage of your home; the result is your business percentage.

Example: Let's assume you live in a two-bedroom apartment of 750 square feet and convert a 10-by-15-foot bedroom into a home office and studio. Multiply the room dimensions to arrive at the square footage (10 feet x 15 feet = 150 square feet). Now divide the square footage of the converted bedroom by the total square footage (150 ÷ 750 = .20). Your allowable deduction is 20 percent. If you live in a house of 3,000 square feet and use 1,000 square feet for business, your allowable deduction is 33.33 percent. You see how it works.

The IRS allows you to use any reasonable method to determine your business percentage. The one I've described is the most accurate and is certainly easy enough.

What You Can Deduct

Expenses associated solely with your living quarters and other areas of your property that have nothing to do with your business are *unrelated expenses* and as such are not deductible. These include repair and maintenance of living quarters and most appliances, landscaping expenses, lawn care, and such.

If you need to repair or replace a dishwasher or range, no portion of the associated costs is deductible. On the other hand, some seemingly unrelated expenses might be deductible. For example, if a major part of your business is darkroom work, you might use as much water in your business as you do in your personal life, in which case repair or replacement of a water heater might be partly deductible.

Costs associated solely with the benefit of your business are known as *direct expenses* and are fully deductible. If you put new carpeting in your office, paint your studio, replace a faulty faucet in your darkroom, or hang a new light fixture in any part of your work area, you may deduct the expenses.

Most of the costs of running and maintaining your entire home are partly deductible as *indirect expenses*. They include mortgage interest, real-estate taxes, utilities, trash collection, some telephone charges, insurance premiums, and security systems.

Casualty losses, depending on their effects, can be unrelated, direct, or indirect expenses and are accordingly deductible or not. A grease fire that damages only your kitchen is a casualty loss but is unrelated to your business and not an allowable business deduction. If a storm blows the windows out of your office, the casualty loss is directly related to your business and is fully deductible, less any insurance compensation. If a tornado delivers your roof to an adjacent county, the loss affects both your business and your living quarters and is treated as an indirect expense, less any insurance or other reimbursement.

If you're a renter who meets all the criteria for the business use of your home, the business percentage of your rent is deductible. If you're a homeowner, however, no portion of your principal payments on your mortgage is deductible, but you should be able to recover these business costs over several years by taking an annual deduction for depreciation of the building and any permanent improvements to it.

Limitations and Reporting Requirements

Your allowable deduction, including depreciation, for the business use of your home is limited. In simplest terms, deductions for the business use of your home are not allowed to exceed your net income. If they do, all or part of the deductions might be disallowed for that year, but those disallowed expenses may be carried over to a later year.

Form 8829, "Expenses for Business Use of Your Home," is where you report all this information and where you will determine whether or not your expenses for any given year are deductible that year.

USING A VEHICLE IN YOUR BUSINESS

It's hard to imagine running a home-based photography business without using a vehicle. Depending on the nature of your work, you may only occasionally need to drive or you might be on the road every day. You might buy a vehicle to use exclusively for business purposes, or you can enlist the family flivver for both business and personal use.

The IRS uses the term *car* to mean any passenger vehicle that does not exceed 6,000 pounds gross vehicle weight. That includes the kinds of vehicles most of us use for transportation: automobiles, vans, minivans, pickup trucks, and sport-utility vehicles.

Near Home and Away

Depending on the kind of photography you do, you might travel only locally or some distance to see to your business needs. Your business-home area includes the metropolitan, suburban, or rural area where you do business during the course of a normal workday or local job or assignment. If you travel to and from a job location within the same day, that's considered local use of your vehicle, and costs associated with such use are deductible as vehicle expenses.

If business takes you away from home overnight or for a longer period, you must consider your vehicle expenses to be part of your *travel* expenses, which are recorded and handled separately and reported in a different section of Schedule C, "Profit or Loss from Business."

According to the IRS, expenses for the local business use of your vehicle are deductible "if the expenses are ordinary and necessary. An ordinary expense is one that is common and accepted in your field of trade, business, or profession. A necessary expense is one that is helpful and appropriate for your business. An expense does not have to be indispensable to be considered necessary."

Vehicle Use Test and Expense Records

If you use a family vehicle for both business and personal purposes, business mileage must amount to more than 50 percent of the total mileage to qualify for the highest depreciation deductions. So you must keep good mileage records. How else could you know that of the 18,500 miles you drove last year, 12,580 were for business, allowing you to deduct 68 percent of your vehicle operating costs?

You should keep a mileage log, but it needn't be anything elaborate. Note the date and odometer mileage when you place a vehicle in service. Then for each trip, show date, destination or purpose, starting odometer mileage, ending mileage, and total mileage.

MILEAGE LOG

DATE	DESTINATION/ PURPOSE	STARTING MILEAGE	ENDING MILEAGE	TOTAL MILEAGE

TOTAL MILEAGE THIS PAGE _____

Your log can be a notebook or a ruled legal- or letter-size pad on a clipboard that you keep in your vehicle. You can also make your mileage log part of your business planner and calendar, either with loose-leaf pages or with printed pages designed for such purposes.

You may elect either to take a standard deduction for each business mile you drive or to deduct actual vehicle expenses and depreciation. In the latter case, you should also keep receipts, work orders, canceled checks, and any other documents that substantiate your claims for expense deductions. There's no requirement to keep a separate diary or journal of vehicle expenses, but you may, if you prefer that to recording expenses in a general expense ledger. In either case, you need not duplicate any information already contained on your receipts and other documents.

Mileage vs Expenses

Whether to take the standard mileage deduction or deduct actual operating expenses is up to you. If your vehicle is cheap to operate, you might be smart to take the mileage deduction. You'll probably be better off deducting operating expenses and depreciation, however, if you drive an expensive gas hog.

In addition to keeping a mileage log, I recommend you record all your operating costs as well for the first year. At tax-filing time, do all the necessary calculations for both methods and pick the one that will give you the greater deduction.

Once you figure the total miles and business miles driven for the year, divide the business miles by the total miles to arrive at your business percentage. For example, if you drive 10,935 business miles and 3,645 personal miles, total mileage for the year is 14,580. If you divide 10,935 by 14,580, you'll find that your business miles constitute 75 percent of the total. That means you can deduct 75 percent of your operating expenses and depreciation, or multiply the standard per-mile deduction by 10,935 and deduct that amount.

Leasing a Vehicle

Another option is to lease a vehicle instead of buying one. With a leased vehicle, you are normally allowed to deduct maintenance and repair bills, operating expenses, and lease payments. You may not use the standard mileage deduction; nor may you deduct for depreciation. You must, however, log business and personal mileage.

Based on the kind of lease agreement you sign, the IRS might require you to treat the leased vehicle as you would a purchased vehicle. If your lease contains an option-to-buy clause, the IRS may consider this a purchase agreement. So be careful with any lease and its wording. You may wish to seek assistance from the IRS or your attorney before signing a vehicle lease.

If the vehicle you lease has what the IRS considers an "excess fair-market value," you will also have to report an "inclusion amount" when you file your tax return. For information about all this, see IRS Publication 917, *Business Use of a Car*, or one of the commercially available tax guides published each year.

Renting a Vehicle

Should your business require you to travel away from your business-home area by public conveyance, such as by plane or train, you might need to rent a vehicle once you reach your business destination. Your rental payments and operating costs are deductible as travel transportation expenses, as are your plane or train tickets.

Other Deductible Expenses

Unless you take the standard mileage deduction, most expenses you incur while operating your vehicle for business purposes are deductible. In addition to fuel, repairs, and maintenance, they include but are not limited to bridge and highway tolls, ferry fees, parking fees, parking-valet gratuities, and towing charges, should your vehicle become disabled.

Fines for moving and parking violations are not deductible; nor are towing charges stemming from illegal parking.

USING A COMPUTER IN YOUR BUSINESS

If you buy a computer that you and other family members use for personal reasons, school work, computer games, and other nonbusiness purposes and you also plan to use it for business, the IRS considers this *listed property*, and you will need to keep track of and distinguish between personal and business use. If your business use is less than 50 percent of the total use, your deductions will be limited.

Logging computer use is more difficult than logging vehicle use, especially if several people use the computer. For that reason and others, I recommend you purchase a computer, put it in your office or studio, and use it exclusively for business. In this case, it is not considered listed property, and you may treat it as any other depreciable business property.

All peripheral computer equipment and hardware and most software are also depreciable property. Blank diskettes (floppy disks), computer paper, printer ribbons or cartridges, labels, and other essential computer materials are deductible as office supplies. (See Chapter 8, "Using a Computer in Your Business.")

BUSINESS EXPENSES

Most of the costs of running your business are fully deductible in a straightforward way. As the sole proprietor of a home-based business, you will have to sort out the various deductions and report them on their respective forms: some on Form 8829, "Expenses for Business Use of Your Home"; some on Schedule C, "Profit or Loss from Business"; and some on Form 4562, "Depreciation and Amortization."

We've already discussed deductions for the business use of your home and will more fully discuss depreciation later. For now, let's take a closer look at the kinds of expenses you will report on Schedule C. They include but are not necessarily limited to expenses incurred for advertising, business operation of a vehicle, interest paid, legal and professional services, materials and supplies, rent, leases, repairs and maintenance, taxes, licenses, permits, travel, some meals, entertainment, dues, some publications, printing and photocopying, postal costs, freight, express and parcel services, lab services, trash collection, and others you'll no doubt discover.

Keeping Records

Keeping receipts is not the chore so many people think it is. Mainly, it's a matter of developing the habit of collecting receipts for all your business purchases.

For most of your expenses, receipts are automatic aspects of your various transactions. Your telephone, utilities, and other monthly bills are receipts you'll need to keep. When you gas up your vehicle, keep the credit-card receipt; if you pay cash, ask for a cash receipt. When you're on the road, get receipts for all your food, lodging, and other expenses.

If you buy office and photography supplies in quantity, you'll keep the number of receipts to a minimum. Set up accounts with vendors and you'll also save time and trouble by paying and filing monthly statements.

Even when you get all this under control, you will still need to buy a roll or two of film, batteries, or other essentials now and then at supermarkets and drugstores. Just make sure you get a cash-register receipt. Many register receipts itemize purchases, and all provide dates and amounts. When you get a register receipt that doesn't display all the essential information, fill it in yourself, immediately.

I make a habit of marking receipts as I get them and noting any important information. I use a red pen to circle the date and amount paid. If the receipt isn't itemized, I write down what it was for: film, photocopies, lunch, and such. This helps me zero in on the information I need when I do my bookkeeping.

When I pay my stacks of monthly bills, I note the date and circle the amount paid, but I don't bother writing the check number on the bill, because that will be in my check register if I need it. While I'm at it, I put a red X in the check register at each check I write to pay for an expense for which I don't have an adequate receipt. The canceled check is then my receipt.

No matter how careful you are, you will sometimes forget to ask for a receipt, or you might lose one. In that case, make your own receipt at once, noting all the pertinent information. This should be acceptable to the IRS. What's important is that you write the receipt while everything is fresh in your mind, not at the end of the month when you do your bookkeeping.

DEPRECIATION OF BUSINESS PROPERTY

The purchase of certain equipment, tools, furnishings, and other property you use in your business is considered a capital expenditure, not normally eligible for deduction as an expense for a given tax year. Rather, it must be treated as depreciable property, with the cost or other basis deducted gradually over a number of years. Normally, this includes any property that has a useful life of more than one year.

In addition to vehicles and computers, already discussed, other depreciable property you will probably use in your home-based photography business includes the following:

- *Furniture and fixtures* for your office, studio, and darkroom.

- *Office equipment*, such as a typewriter, calculator, copier, fax machine, and telephone.

- *Photography equipment*, including cameras, lenses, flash units, and tripods.

- *Studio equipment*, such as floodlights, strobes, light stands, background stands, and duplicating equipment.

- *Darkroom equipment*, including an enlarger, enlarger lenses, safelights, and a print dryer.

- *Buildings* not used for residential purposes, including the business portion of your home.

Property Classes and Recovery Periods

Various depreciable property is classified according to the number of years you must normally take to depreciate it or write it off. Because of conventions you're required to use in calculating depreciation, recovery periods run a year longer than their respective classifications. For example, so-called *five-year property* will remain on your books for six years, *seven-year property* for eight.

Any machinery you use—including office and photography equipment, computer equipment, and vehicles—is five-year property. Desks, chairs, filing cabinets, bookcases, tables, and other furniture and fixtures you use in your business are seven-year property.

Congress keeps extending the recovery period for nonresidential real property. In 1993 it was increased from thirty-one and a half years to thirty-nine years. By the time you read this, it could be even longer. The annual deductible rate for thirty-nine-year real property is 2.5641 percent, except for prorated first and last years.

Section-179 Deductions

Here's an exception to what we've been discussing. Certain tangible personal property used in business is eligible to be treated as an expense and may be fully or partly deductible for the tax year. You may deduct up to $17,500 of the cost of such property as office equipment, computers, peripherals, and photography gear.

Your business vehicle is eligible, provided it was not previously used as a personal vehicle and then converted to business use. The Section-179 deduction for qualifying vehicles is also limited.

Buildings are not eligible for Section-179 deductions.

You can use this information to your advantage by paying close attention to your earnings and expenses. If you have a better year than you anticipated, you might need all the immediate deductions you can legally take to reduce your taxable income. That's a good time to look for possible Section-179 deductions. If your income turns out lower than you expect, and you have plenty of deductions, you probably won't want to take the Section-179 deductions, even if you have purchased eligible property. Normal depreciation procedures will extend your deductions into future years, when, presumably, your income will be higher.

Reporting Depreciation

Enter all pertinent depreciation information on Form 4562, "Depreciation and Amortization." Once you have calculated your allowable depreciation, you'll enter the total on Schedule C.

Surmounting all the obstacles and wading through the mire of instructions for figuring depreciation can make for a difficult trip. This single aspect of taxation might be troublesome enough to make you seek the services of a tax professional.

If you want to try it on your own, you should consult IRS Publication 334, *Tax Guide for Small Business,* and Publication 534, *Depreciation.* Some of the commercially available guides, such as *J. K. Lasser's Your Income Tax* and *H&R Block Income Tax Guide*, are eminently more readable and relatively free of bureaucratic gobbledegook.

ESTIMATING YOUR TAXES

Uncle Sam doesn't like to have money owed to him at the end of the year, so we're required to keep our taxes paid up. In a simpler, saner system, it would be easy to do the bookkeeping at the end of the month, deduct a reasonable percentage from profits, and mail the old guy a check. But Uncle also dislikes simple and sane systems. So we have yet another form to fill out and another exercise in exasperation.

If you're working part-time at this business and full-time elsewhere, you can increase the amount your employer withholds from your paycheck to keep from owing taxes at year's end. You could have a working spouse do the same, if you file jointly. Otherwise, you will have to estimate your income and taxes, file Form 1040-ES, and pay your estimated taxes quarterly.

RECORD KEEPING

As a self-employed taxpayer, you may use either the accrual or the cash accounting basis. With the accrual basis, you report income as it is earned, not as it's received. You also report expenses on the dates you incur them, not necessarily on the day you pay them. On a cash basis, you report income when you are paid and costs as you pay them.

Advantages of Cash Basis

Cash accounting is certainly the simpler method. It also offers certain advantages that can save you tax dollars. For example, at the end of a high-income year, you may elect to delay your billing until late December or early January in order to defer payment of money owed you into the coming tax year, thus reducing your taxable income for the current year.

No Set Rules for Records

You must keep accurate records of all your income and all your expenditures. There are no set IRS requirements, however, for how you set up your books, so long as you maintain written records or computer records you can print out.

You can turn over your record-keeping chores to a professional, or do it yourself. You might want to visit an office-supply outlet to examine available commercial accounting and record-keeping systems, or devise something yourself. If you own a computer, you may wish to review some of the many software programs available for business and personal financial management and record keeping. Some are available as shareware, which you can try for a minimal charge, often as little as $5.00 per disk.

Depending on the nature of your business and how it is physically set up, you might find that keeping computerized records saves time. Among the dozens of software programs available, *Quicken* seems to be the most popular for personal and small-business financial management. It also appears to be the most widely available and among the cheapest, regularly selling for under $50.

A Simple Bookkeeping System

I use a simple manual system I devised when I first went into business part-time. It has served me well for years, keeps me informed, and is housed in a single three-ring loose-leaf binder, which is organized with index-tab pages. The ledger pages are created from my handy-dandy four-column pads.

To keep track of income, I label the top of a page Income, followed by the year. The narrow left column is labeled Date, the wide column Source, and the four accounting columns, respectively, Amount, Month, Total for Month, and Cumulative Total.

As checks arrive, I enter date, source, and amount. At month's end, I write the month in the second column, income for the month in the third column, and a running cumulative total in the fourth column. I record all reimbursed expenses the same way on a page that's identical, except for title.

For recording most of my expenses, my ledger has index tabs and pages labeled Vehicle, Office, Repairs & Maintenance, Dues & Publications, Photo Supplies, Printing & Photocopying, Postal, Freight & Shipping, and Miscellaneous. For each of these categories, I prepare the page with Date in the far-left column and Item in the wide column. I then identify the four accounting columns Cost, Month, Total for Month, and Cumulative Total.

Several categories call for special handling. For example, my Travel & Entertainment pages reflect certain IRS requirements as well as my own needs to see how I spend my money. I label the four accounting columns Meals & Entertainment, Transportation, Lodging, and Miscellaneous. After each trip I subtotal each column. The IRS allows a deduction for

INCOME/EXPENSES

DATE	SOURCE OR ITEM	AMOUNT OR COST	MONTH	TOTAL FOR MONTH	CUMULATIVE TOTAL

only a percentage of meals and entertainment, which the ledger page keeps separate.

On another page, titled Utilities, Phone, & Trash, I label the wide column Month, under which I list the twelve months. The four columns are for Electric, Water, Phone, and Trash. Totals for electric, water, and trash get adjusted by my business percentage. I adjust my phone charges as I review my monthly bills.

If you have only one phone line coming into your home, the IRS does not allow a deduction for that line but does allow the deduction of long-distance calls. If you put a second line into your office, or a dedicated fax line, you may deduct charges for them.

I have four insurance policies that are directly or indirectly related to my business. The insurance page in my ledger has columns for Vehicle, Boat, Homeowner, and Mortgage. I report costs for my vehicle and boat insurance on Schedule C, adjusted homeowner's and mortgage insurance on Form 8829.

For depreciation, I make ledger pages for various kinds of property. Although I could keep all five-year property together and all seven-year property together, I prefer to further categorize. For example, I have pages labeled Books & Software (5-Year Property), Machinery & Equipment (5-Year Property), and Furniture & Fixtures (7-Year Property). I also keep the records for my business vehicle on a separate sheet, labeled Vehicle (5-Year Property).

The far-left column of each depreciation page is labeled Date, the wide column Item, and the first accounting column Cost. I leave the other columns untitled until year end. If I elect to expense any of these items as a Section-179 deduction, I so note it on the page for future reference. If I depreciate property, I then use the other columns, showing the current year and percentage allowed at the head of column two. The following year, I enter the year and percentage at the head of column three, and the year after in column four. Sometimes there's sufficient room to continue adding the out years at the bottom of the same page. When there's not, I just add another page.

I try to keep up with all this by doing my bookkeeping monthly, but sometimes I'm too busy and must put off the job for a month or so. At the end of the year, I run my column totals and do all the necessary calculating to make my books ready for filling out my tax forms.

USEFUL PUBLICATIONS FROM THE IRS

Number	Title
17	Your Federal Income Tax
334	Tax Guide for Small Business
463	Travel, Entertainment, and Gift Expenses
505	Tax Withholding and Estimated Tax
521	Moving Expenses
523	Tax Information on Selling Your House
525	Taxable and Nontaxable Income
526	Charitable Contributions
533	Self-Employment Tax
534	Depreciation
535	Business Expenses
536	Net Operating Losses
538	Accounting Periods and Methods
541	Tax Information on Partnerships
542	Tax Information on Corporations
544	Sales and Other Dispositions of Assets
550	Investment Income and Expenses
551	Basis of Assets
553	Highlights of [the Year's] Tax Changes
560	Retirement Plans for the Self-Employed
561	Determining the Value of Donated Property
583	Taxpayers Starting a Business
587	Business Use of Your Home
589	Tax Information on S Corporations
590	Individual Retirement Arrangements (IRAs)
917	Business Use of a Car
946	How to Begin Depreciating Your Property

IRS FORMS YOU'LL PROBABLY NEED

Number	Title
Form 1040	U.S. Individual Income Tax Return
Form 1040-ES	Estimated Tax for Individuals
Form 4562	Depreciation and Amortization
Form 8829	Expenses for Business Use of Your Home
Schedule A	Itemized Deductions
Schedule B	Interest and Dividend Income
Schedule C	Profit or Loss from Business
Schedule D	Capital Gains and Losses
Schedule SE	Self-Employment Tax

CAPITALIZING START-UP COSTS

To allow for a deduction of the preliminary costs of starting a business, the IRS requires those costs to be capitalized over time. Some of these costs might not be deductible until the business terminates. All of this can lead to some complicated and time-consuming record keeping.

For big companies making major investments in equipment and materials, the record keeping and procedures are necessary for taking the concomitantly large deductions. For the home-based entrepreneur, however, the puny deductions are hardly worth the hassles.

You can simply elect not to take deductions for start-up costs. You won't have to do all that bookkeeping, and you won't run afoul of IRS regulations. But make sure you keep your start-up costs low. Anything you buy before you're in business is the kind of expenditure that would have to be capitalized to be eligible for deduction. Once you've made a sale, however, you are officially in business and may then begin deducting expenses in the same tax year they occur.

Of course, you will want to use tools and materials you already have on hand; you just shouldn't take deductions for them if you want to avoid the capitalization hassles.

My recommendation is to keep your start-up costs minimal and to make a sale as soon as possible. Don't buy new office furniture and equipment or lay in large quantities of materials and supplies before you've sold anything. Operate on a shoestring until you make a sale; then begin purchasing the necessities for your business, keeping all the receipts and maintaining careful records of all expenditures.

SALES TAX

Depending on the nature of your business and your state's requirements, you might have to apply for a license to collect sales tax on the items you sell.

If your state has a sales tax, you might have to collect taxes on items you sell directly to customers at arts-and-crafts shows, craft fairs, and similar events. On the other hand, you probably won't have to collect taxes items you sell through shops, galleries, stores, or any other retail outlets where the proprietors of those businesses collect taxes from their customers. Similarly, you should be exempt from paying sales taxes on raw materials and finished products that you purchase for resale. The idea here is to prevent what would amount to multiple taxation on the product as it progresses through the stages of manufacture.

You'll need to determine your state's requirements. So check at your local chamber of commerce or Small Business Development Center. You can also get information from your state revenue department.

CHAPTER EIGHT

USING A COMPUTER IN YOUR BUSINESS

I f you're an intermediate to advanced computer user, you can probably skip this chapter, because you already know more about computers than I do. I'm no computer expert and wouldn't dare to pretend to be. I'm merely a home-based business owner and manager who relies on computers for an ever-increasing number of business tasks.

If you've had only minimal experience with personal computers, or none at all, perhaps I can be of some service. I've learned a thing or two over the years, often the hard way, that may assist you in determining your computer needs.

Like many other busy entrepreneurs, I came reluctantly to the computer world after much deliberation and the discovery of two important reasons for computerizing my business. First, doing so made good business sense. Second, I was about to be left in the dust by a growing number of computerized colleagues and competitors.

Have I had any regrets about my decision? Only one: that I didn't have the good sense and foresight to make the move years before I did. So learn from my big mistake, allay any fears you might have, climb aboard, and enjoy the electronic ride more than you might think.

GETTING STARTED WITH A COMPUTER

The first notion you must dispel is that you need to be a mathematical genius, an electronic whiz, or a nine-year-old child to successfully grasp the intricacies of computer operation. The second notion to put to rest is that a computer is a magic machine that will solve all your business problems.

If you possess enough manual dexterity to operate an electronic calculator or electric typewriter, you can learn your way around a computer's keyboard. If you can read and comprehend at a seventh-grade level, you'll have little trouble learning and understanding the commands essential to the operation of a computer and the functions of hardware and software.

I didn't say you're going to understand, much less enjoy, all the documentation that comes with computer hardware and software. Some of it is written by computer eggheads whose native tongue is jargon and who venture into short phrases of plain English only by accident. You've met them before. They wrote the instructions on how to program your VCR and the manual on how to operate your new auto-everything camera.

The good news is that there are some computer experts who speak and write English and have the ability to translate all that computerese into readable and informative books and magazine articles. Without their help, my own computer would be functioning as little more than an expensive typewriter.

A computer won't improve your photographic skills or make you a better bookkeeper or business communicator. But it can reduce the time it takes to perform tasks associated with your photography and your business, thereby freeing you to increase your productivity or learn more about the art, craft, and business of photography.

Increased productivity is probably the most important benefit you'll gain from computerizing your business, but it won't be immediate. In fact, you'll probably lose a few days to setting up your system and learning how to use it. You'll have to spend more time mastering the basics and learning what you need to know about various computer applications. You will soon reach a point, however, when you are comfortable with the hardware and software and will begin saving time on various tasks.

What a Computer Can Do for Your Business

In considering the computerization of your home-based business, think of the computer as your assistant manager. You can delegate many tasks to this able helpmate, such as the management of correspondence, accounts, billing, inventory, files, data, money, and time.

You can even assign your assistant all the phone chores, from dialing up customers to answering the phone and routing incoming calls to their proper destinations. Your computer can send and receive faxes and even take messages in your absence. You say you have to leave the office for awhile but are expecting some important calls? If you own the right software, just leave the number where you can be reached and your computer will forward your calls. Your computer can communicate with other computers around the world.

You can hook up by modem to on-line services and networks. You can subscribe to bulletin-board services (BBSs) in your business and interest areas, engage in discussions with your colleagues, get answers to your questions, download information, and much more.

Master the Jargon

When you're trying to learn anything about anything, from aeroballistics to zymology, the first order of business is to learn the peculiar terminology of the discipline. If you don't know what all the terms, abbreviations, and acronyms mean, you can't expect to learn from what you read and hear.

The computer world is full of jargon, which can be terribly frustrating to those trying to learn about computers on an elementary level. I suggest that before you try to read a magazine article or book about computers, you invest in a good computer dictionary, such as the *Dictionary of Computer Terms,* Third Edition, by Douglas Downing and Michael Covington (Barron's, 1992). This inexpensive, compact volume is small enough to keep handy at all times.

When you encounter any term you don't understand, look it up. You'll soon be breezing through computer articles and books with no trouble.

Learn by Reading

Armed with your handy-dandy dictionary, you should be ready to learn by reading computer books and magazines. Visit local libraries, bookstores, and magazine stands to see what's available and what might be most appealing and valuable to you and your business.

The first book you should look for is *How to Computerize Your Small Business,* by Patrick D. O'Hara (John Wiley & Sons, Inc., 1993). This eminently readable and informative book will prove a tremendous help in determining what you need in the way of a computer system, how to set it all up, how to install your software, and how to put all this to work for you.

I wish O'Hara's book had been available when I bought my first computer system. Although I think I would have ended up with the same system I eventually decided on, this book would have saved me time and trouble and provided knowledge and confidence I lacked. Consider this one your start-up bible, and read it before you buy your system.

You'll get some basic information about your disk operating system (DOS) from O'Hara's book, which is probably all you'll need for that aging system. New personal computer systems now come loaded with Windows 95, so you would do well to bone up on that operating system instead of spending time trying to wade through the intricacies of MS-DOS. A good choice is *Teach Yourself Windows 95,* by Al Stevens.

IDG Books publishes a series of understandable books about personal computers and software, including *DOS for Dummies,* by Dan Gookin. If you end up buying a Macintosh system, you'll probably want to read *Macs for Dummies* and *More Macs for Dummies,* by David Pogue.

Match other IDG offerings with the software that comes with your computer system and any mainstream applications you add later on. You'll find *Dummies* titles for Windows, WordPerfect, Word, Ami Pro, Excel, 1-2-3, Quicken, the Internet, and more.

If you decide on WordPerfect as your word-processing program, I can recommend *WordPerfect 6 Made Easy,* by Mella Mincberg (Osborne/McGraw-Hill, 1993).

Well-written books provide an excellent way to learn about computers and software and serve afterward as valuable reference volumes, but you will also need to read computer magazines to keep up with the rapidly changing technology. Although you'll find a bewildering variety of computer magazines available, you can narrow the selection first by eliminating all the specialized periodicals that deal with hardware and software you don't own, then by examining others to find those you like most.

The first computer magazine I subscribed to was *PC Magazine.* After two years, however, I let the subscription lapse, not because the magazine disappointed me in any way but because it was simply too much material coming at me too fast. Regardless of how informative and generally well written *PC Magazine* is, 800 pages of editorial and advertising every two weeks is a bit more than I can handle and still keep up with all the reading and research I must do on photography.

PC World is less than half the size of *PC Magazine*, but at more than 300 pages a month, it's still a tremendous amount of material to cover, considering this is just one of many magazines I read. So I've let that subscription lapse, too. I regularly browse through these magazines at the newsstand, however, and buy issues of each when the magazines cover something of particular interest and relevance to me. *Computer Shopper* is another huge magazine I buy at the newsstand.

Of the specialty magazines, I continue to subscribe to *Home Office Computing* because it is well written and relates to my business. I also take *WordPerfect* magazine as a way of learning more about that powerful word-processing program and keeping up with the latest technology.

What I find particularly valuable in *PC Magazine* and *PC World* are their exhaustive tests of hardware and classes of hardware. I bought my first computer system based largely on the testing and evaluation of more than forty similar systems by *PC Magazine*. The magazines' editors regularly run such tests on desktop computers, notebooks, printers, and other hardware. Keep watch for these issues; you'll learn a lot from them.

Take Computer Courses

One of the best ways to learn about computers is to enroll in basic computer courses. Those who don't have the time to spend an entire semester in a course might find the intensive one-day or weekend workshops more to their liking.

You'll find computer courses offered at local universities and colleges, community colleges, trade schools, computer schools, and some computer stores. Phone or write for university and college catalogs and any literature the trade and computer schools offer. Visit local computer stores to learn what they have available, and ask to be put on their mailing lists for courses and workshops.

Some computer and software companies also offer seminars and workshops that can be helpful. Many of these are traveling programs, offered at major population centers in all regions of the United States. Watch for local advertisements and announcements, or phone the companies to inquire about their instructional programs.

The TV-VCR Connection

Check your TV listings to determine whether your local affiliate of the Public Broadcasting System runs *The Computer Chronicles*. This excellent weekly program has provided me with an abundance of useful information and introduced me to many interesting computer applications. My wife records the programs for me so I can watch them at my leisure.

Also check local video-rental and computer stores, many of which carry instructional videos about computers and software. You should find other videos you can borrow free at your local public library.

Befriend a Nerd

Ask my kid brother what he does for a living and he'll unabashedly tell you he's a computer nerd. Actually, he's a musician with his own band, a degree in journalism, and plans for graduate work. He's also a qualified diesel and small-engine mechanic and a pretty fair carpenter, but his field of expertise is computer and sound-system consulting.

Inasmuch as he still resides in Alaska and I now live a half-continent farther south, I can pick his brain only by long distance. Luckily, though, there seems to be no shortage of hackers to go around. One friend of mine is an electrical engineer who taught himself to be a computer expert. Another friend is a retired Air Force computer programmer who teaches computer courses and specializes in DOS and WordPerfect. He and I live in different cities, but we're able to communicate quickly and easily by e-mail, which also puts me in touch with many other experts.

Chances are, you already have at least one friend who knows a lot about computers and software. And you'll surely get to know others who will gladly offer advice. What you learn from these folks can prove invaluable.

You'll also want to find out about computer experts in your vicinity who work as consultants on an hourly basis. Sometimes an hour's worth of a consultant's time can save you untold hours of grief.

HARDWARE OVERVIEW

The basic computer system for a home-based business consists of a keyboard, printer, and monitor attached by cables to a case that houses the brains of the whole outfit: the microprocessor, which is an integrated circuit that contains the central processing unit (CPU) on a single chip. The CPU is what controls the computer and where instructions are executed and various operations are carried out. Also inside the case are the computer's memory and input-output devices.

Microprocessors

The first microprocessor was Intel's 8088, introduced in 1973. Since then, Intel has introduced succeeding generations of microprocessors that have bested their predecessors in phenomenal leaps, as measured in terms of power and speed or in the amount of data they can process and the speed with which they move it. Other Intel microprocessor designations have been the 8086, 80286, 80386, 80486, Pentium, and P-6. Earlier generations are commonly referred to by their abbreviated designations: 286, 386, and 486.

The speed of a microprocessor is measured in megahertz (MHz); 1 MHz is a million cycles per second. Every instruction takes several cycles, and microprocessors are capable of working at millions of cycles per second. This speed is referred to as clock speed. Generally, when measured in terms of identical machine instructions, higher clock speeds result in greater computation speeds. But differences can exist between two microprocessors of the same family performing the same computations, simply because one computer might be set up differently from the other. In other words, two 486 microprocessors operating at 33MHz might carry out the same instructions at different speeds. Also, succeeding generations perform faster.

As I write this, current-configuration computers sold by the various computer companies are mostly based on Pentium microprocessors. Although you'll no doubt find plenty of the 80286 and 80386 computers for sale as used equipment, these old workhorses are now considered obsolete, made so by hundreds of new applications that they are incapable of running or are so slow at running as to be impractical. For example, it's possible to run Windows and Windows-based applications on a 286 computer that has sufficient hard-drive and memory capacity, but you'll grow old staring at the monitor waiting for things to happen. With Windows 95, you'd better have a fast 486 or Pentium processor.

I recently bought a new computer system, but not until I'd spent so much time studying options and putting off buying that the whole 486 generation had whizzed right by. What I ended up with is a 100MHz Pentium system that should easily see to my needs for the foreseeable future. I wanted a system that could accommodate imaging tasks, desktop publishing (DTP), computer-assisted design (CAD), and other computation-intensive applications with ease and speed. I also needed hardware that would quickly navigate in the Windows 95 environment, and that's what I got.

So depending on your software needs—and that's exactly what you should base your decision on—you will probably want to seriously consider a system based on one of the Pentium processors. Some bargain packages are available for under $1,500, and you should be able to get into a powerful Pentium system for under $3,000.

Hard Drives

Just as minimal requirements for power and speed keep increasing, so too does the need for hard-drive capacity. The hard disk is where you will store your applications. You might want to store data there as well.

There was a time when 80MB seemed a phenomenal capacity for a hard disk, and most of us figured we could get by for years with something so huge. Who would have imagined that Corel's latest version of WordPerfect Suite for Windows 95 would take up more than 100MB and that most Windows-based applications would eat up 15MB or more apiece?

The usual suggestion is to get as big a hard drive as you can afford, and now the experts are telling us we'd better consider 500MB the minimum. Drives as big as 1 gigabyte (1,000MB), and even larger, are now common on many configurations.

Diskette (Floppy) Drives

Most computers now come with one 3½-inch density diskette or floppy-disk drive, but the older 5¼-inch drives are still available as add-on equipment for those who need them.

A double-sided, high density (DS/HD) 5 5¼-inch floppy disk can store up to 1.2MB of data. A DS/HD 3 3½-inch diskette can store up to 1.44MB, or the equivalent of two books the size of this one, with room to spare.

Memory

Random-access memory (RAM) is another important consideration in the purchase of any computer. My first computer came with 512KB of RAM, expandable to 4MB. Now, with Windows 95 and its memory-hungry applications, 8MB is the minimum you can get by with, and the recommendation is to go with at least 16MB, which you can increase later. Typical Pentium configurations offer 8MB or 16MB of RAM, expandable to 128MB. Depending on the microprocessor you buy and the software you use, the difference between 8MB and 16MB of RAM can be the difference between ambling and sprinting through some applications.

Monitors

Most monitors now sold with computer systems have 14- or 15-inch screens, although larger screens are available and recommended for more intensive graphics applications.

Monitor performance and quality are variable among the monitors and video-adapter cards available. What you need in a monitor and video package depends largely on what you want your system to do.

The capability of any video card is expressed in terms of the number of colors offered and resolution. The minimum recommended for many current DOS applications is 256 colors and resolution of 640 by 480. For Windows it's 256 colors and 800-by-600 resolution.

For Windows and other graphics-intensive applications, you should have a graphic accelerator card installed in your computer to speed things up.

In your search for the right monitor, you will no doubt encounter the term *refresh rate*. This refers to the way the monitor scans or paints the image onto the screen. The refresh rate is expressed in cycles per second (Hz)—the higher the better—and 70Hz to 72Hz is recommended. Lower refresh rates can cause the screen to flicker.

Interlaced and *noninterlaced* are two other monitor terms you should know about. The interlaced monitors paint every other horizontal line as they scan the screen from top to bottom; they then vertically scan a second time to fill in the remaining lines. Noninterlaced monitors paint the screen in a single swipe and thus eliminate the irritating flicker associated with the cheaper interlaced monitors.

There's much more to video and graphics considerations than you might think, and an abundance of confusing terminology doesn't help the decision-making process. What's more, it's difficult to determine your needs by reading magazine articles and product tests. You must see the differences among the various monitor and video-adapter combinations to appreciate them. Visit local computer stores and ask for demonstrations.

Printers

These days you'll have a choice of three types of printers: dot matrix, inkjet, and laser. Dot-matrix printers are the least expensive, lasers the most expensive, though their prices have dropped significantly enough to make them a good choice for many home-based businesses.

A 24-pin dot matrix will see to most or all of your business needs, providing you don't need publication-quality documents. If you need to produce wide documents and multipart forms, dot matrix is your only choice. It's also a good printer to start with and to keep even if you later invest in an inkjet or laser printer. You should be able to find a good 24-pin model for under $300.

For higher-quality documents, inkjet printers are a good compromise between dot-matrix and laser printers. Their prices range from about $300 to $500.

Laser printers are expensive, ranging from about $500 to $1,000 or more. When you need printing of the highest quality, though, these are the machines that provide it. I recently added a laser printer to my system, and it was delivered to my doorstep for $499, including overnight shipping charges.

Peripheral Considerations

Peripherals are simply devices attached to a computer and include disk drives, tape drives, and modems. Some are designed for external attachment, others for internal installation. Whenever possible, buy internal peripherals to conserve desktop space. They're fairly easy to install, so you can do the job yourself. If you're uncomfortable with the idea of removing the cover and poking around inside your computer, hire someone to install the peripherals for you. You can have the job done on site, but it will cost less to haul your computer and peripherals to a local computer shop and have it done there.

It's always cheaper to buy or upgrade peripherals at the time you purchase a computer system. Your dealer or manufacturer should also be able to install the add-ons for a nominal labor charge.

My current system includes a CD-ROM, which stands for compact disc, read-only memory. A single CD can hold hundreds of megabytes of data, far more than the typical hard drive. It can hold a thousand times as much as a floppy disk, yet store it in about the same amount of space. Some experts assure us that CDs could eventually replace hard disks and diskettes.

When I ordered my Pentium system, I included a tape drive for backup. Backing up a big hard disk can take dozens of diskettes and a lot of time, whereas a single tape can backup 250MB or more in one fell swoop. With compression, some tape drives can backup more than a gigabyte on a single tape cartridge.

SOFTWARE OVERVIEW

Software is what makes a computer work. Without software, a computer is useless, incapable of functioning. Software can be divided into two primary categories: systems and applications.

Your computer will come with operating-system software, such as Windows 95 or Macintosh System 7, already installed. This is the software that controls the computer, manages memory, formats disks and diskettes, and enables the user to create, copy, move, and erase files, as well as run applications software.

Applications software sets up your system to do specific jobs, such as word processing, spreadsheets, accounting, desktop publishing, CAD, drawing, painting, and digital imaging. With the right applications software, your computer can print all kinds of graphics and forms, see to billing chores, track negatives and transparencies, address envelopes and labels, create calendars and to-do lists, remind you about meetings and appointments, and help with bookkeeping, taxes, and check writing. Software can teach your system to do calligraphy, sign your name, and even prepare correspondence and other documents in your own digitized handwriting.

Before deciding on any computer system, you must determine the kinds of applications software you want to run; then customize your system around the requirements of the software. Your computer will come with some software, and by shopping around you might find package deals with software bundles that include all or most of the name-brand software you want.

Some software manufacturers offer basic, inexpensive, all-inclusive packages of integrated software, often priced under $50. Part of the software bundle that came with my first computer was a dandy package called Better Working Eight-in-One. It included a surprisingly good word processor, spreadsheet, outliner, and database, as well as graphics, communications, desktop, and utility programs. There's no better way to get started with a computer and learn your way around various applications than with inexpensive integrated software. You'll learn your money's worth in a hurry.

Some of the big-time software manufacturers are now offering their top titles grouped in "suites" that sometimes sell for not much more than the cost of any single program in the suite. In the suite called Microsoft Office, for example, you get that company's top-flight applications: Word (word processor), Excel (spreadsheet), Access (database), PowerPoint (presentation graphics), and Mail (e-mail). Lotus's SmartSuite includes Word Pro (word processor), 1-2-3 (spreadsheet), Approach (database), Freelance Graphics (presentation graphics), and Organizer (personal information manager). Some high-end systems come loaded with these suites as well as other useful software.

Regardless of what your individual photography and business needs are, certain categories of applications software are essential to most, if not all, businesses. At the top of the list is word processing. Spreadsheets and heavy-duty accounting programs are essential elements in the corporate world but are often too much for the home-based business, where simpler financial programs are usually better and easier to use. Other programs can help you manage your time and put it to better use.

Word Processing

Every business needs to communicate with customers, vendors, and other businesses and individuals. Word-processing software tremendously simplifies that job, allowing the user to turn a computer into an electronic wonder machine for writing and editing letters, news releases, articles, sidebars, captions, reports, brochures, newsletters, and other documents.

My best friend's wife heads up the computer division of the college where she teaches, and she was a tremendous help to me when I bought my first computer system. She knew I needed heavy-duty word-processing capabilities and said I couldn't go wrong with any of the big three, which then were WordStar, WordPerfect, and Microsoft Word. Since then, Lotus's Word Pro has arrived to give the others a run for their money. I went with WordPerfect and have had no regrets.

You'll find less expensive word-processing software available that you might want to try first, especially if your word-processing needs are minimal.

Business Office and Finance Software

Entries for office and finance software ranging from high-priced and powerful spreadsheets to simple bookkeeping programs are available on a trial basis as shareware for less than $5.00 per disk.

If you have lots of numbers to track and manage, by all means consider one of the top-brand spreadsheet programs, such as Lotus 1-2-3 or Microsoft Excel. Otherwise, you can probably get by very well with the simpler and cheaper Quicken, a personal-finance program that many have adapted for small-business use. From the same company comes QuickBooks, a simple and easy-to-use bookkeeping program designed for small business.

If you want electronic help creating your business plan, you should be interested in BizPlanBuilder, available from Power Up! Direct and Egghead Software. From those same sources you'll also find software for creating forms, address books, desk calendars, and to-do lists.

You'll also find software designed to help you with your income taxes, such as J. K. Lasser's Your Income Tax; TurboTax, available from PC Connection; and Tax Mate, from Parsons Technology.

BUYING A COMPUTER SYSTEM

For most of us, houses and vehicles represent our largest purchases. Computers occupy a spot on the list well below boats, motorcycles, lawn tractors, and any number of other expensive items used for work or fun. If we were to evaluate such purchases, however, in terms of complexity, confusion, and frustration, instead of cost, computers would certainly rank in the top three. For many of us they would shake out as number one.

Regardless of where you buy a computer system—from a direct-sales (mail/phone-order) company or local store—you will need to study and evaluate your many options. Even after you've done all your homework and think you know what you want, you'll probably experience more than a little difficulty dealing with all the configurations, combinations, and permutations the various companies offer.

In my own search for a Pentium system, my reading, research, and phone calls eventually narrowed the field to three of the top-rated direct-sales companies. Trying to make intelligent decisions in the face of dozens of configuration options was exasperating. Juggling all the figures and features became remarkably easier, though, when I designed a simple form for comparing the various makes and models.

To use my "Computer Systems Comparison," make a copy of the form, and fill in your minimum system requirements in the left column. Then make enough copies for all the system configurations you're researching.

In the blank box at the top of the form, write in the brand name and configuration of the system under consideration. Show the configured system's price at the bottom of the form. In the center column, fill in the system's standard hardware, software, peripherals, and features. In the right column, list any upgrades and options of interest and their cost. Then it's a simple matter of running the figures, adding shipping and other costs, and arriving at a total system price.

You'll be amazed at how this simple form helps you sort out the profusion of confusion that accompanies the purchase of a new computer system.

COMPUTER AND SOFTWARE SOURCES

After spending a little time with computer magazines, contact the manufacturers of those computers that seem best suited to your needs. The eas-

COMPUTER SYSTEMS COMPARISON

	MINIMUM REQUIREMENTS	CONFIGURED SYSTEM	UPGRADES AND OPTIONS
Processor			
RAM			
Cache			
Hard Drive			
Diskette Drive			
CD-ROM Drive			
Multimedia			
Tape Backup			
Monitor			
Video Card			
DRAM or VRAM			
Fax/Modem			
Case			
Printer			
Warranty			
DOS/Windows			
Software			

Configured System $ _____   Shipping $ _____

Options & Upgrades $ _____   Other Costs $ _____

Installation $ _____   Total for System $ _____

COMPUTER SYSTEMS COMPARISON

	Gateway 2000 P-5 100		

	MINIMUM REQUIREMENTS	CONFIGURED SYSTEM	UPGRADES AND OPTIONS
Processor	75MHz Pentium	100MHz Pentium	
RAM	16MB	16MB	
Cache	256KB	256KB Pipeline Burst	
Hard Drive	1GB	1.2GB	
Diskette Drive	3.5" and 5.25"	3.5"	Combo—$70
CD-ROM Drive	4X	6X	
Multimedia	16-bit Sound Card ACS-40 Speakers		16-bit Wavetable $155
Tape Backup	1GB		1.36GB—$199
Monitor	15" Noninterlaced	15" Noninterlaced	
Video Card	PCI Local Bus	PCI Local Bus	
DRAM or VRAM	1MB	2MB DRAM	
Fax/Modem	14.4K-Baud		28.8K-Baud—$149
Case	Mini Tower	Desktop	Tower—$50
Printer			
Warranty	1-Year	1-Year On-Site 3-Year Limited	
DOS/Windows	Windows 95	Windows 95, Bookshlf MS Office 95 Pro	
Software			
ACS-400 Speakers			$120

Configured System	$ 2,199.00	Shipping	$ 95.00
Options & Upgrades	$ 743.00	Other Costs	$
Installation	$	Total for System	$ 3,037.00

COMPUTER COMPANIES: A TO Z

Aberdeen Inc. (800) 552-6868

Acer America Corp. (800) 239-2237

ACMA Computers Inc. (800) 786-6888

Advanced Logic Research Inc. (800) 444-4257

All Computer Warehouse (800) 775-1953

AMAX Engineering Corp. (800) 800-6328

Apple Computer (800) 732-5151

Compaq Computer Corp. (800) 345-1518

Comtrade (800) 969-2123

Data Storage Inc. (800) 543-6090

Dell Computer Corp. (800) 433-8110

DFI (800) 808-4334

Diamond Technologies Inc. (800) 989-7253

Digital Equipment Corp. (800) 642-4532

Direct Wave Inc. (800) 882-8108

DTK Computer Inc. (800) 289-2385

Empac International (510) 683-8800

Epson America (800) 289-3776

EPS Technologies Inc. (800) 447-0921

Ergo Computing Inc. (800) 880-1925

First Computer Systems Inc. (800) 325-1911

Gateway 2000 Inc. (800) 846-2000

GST/Micro City Inc. (800) 567-2764

Hertz Computer Corp. (800) 232-8737

Hewlett-Packard Co. (800) 322-4772

HiQ Computer Systems (800) 827-5836

IBM PC Direct (800) 426-2968

IPC Technologies Inc. (800) 752-1577

Initiative Technology Inc. (800) 999-1413

Maximus Computers (800) 888-6294

Mega Computer Systems (800) 338-6628

Micron Electronics (800) 388-6334

MidWest Micro (800) 871-9127

MiTAC Corp. (800) 756-9888

Mitsuba Corp. (800) 648-7822

Multiwave Technology (800) 234-3358

NEC Technologies Inc. (800) 632-4636

NETiS Technology Inc. (800) 577-7526

PerComp Microsystems Inc. (800) 856-6688

Polywell Computers Inc. (800) 999-1278

Premio Express Inc. (800) 834-4558

Quantex Microsystems Inc. (800) 613-2047

Robotech Inc. (800) 533-0633

Summit Micro Design Inc. (800) 288-5828

Sys Technology (800) 613-9963

Tagram Systems Corp. (800) 824-7267

Tangent Computer Inc. (800) 974-6658

Tatung Company of America Inc. (800) 829-2850

Toshiba America (800) 457-7777

Unisys Corp. (800) 448-1424

Unitek Technology Inc. (800) 944-5650

USA Flex Inc. (800) 872-3539

Vektron (800) 725-0009

Wedge Technology Inc. (800) 872-9334

Zenith Data Systems (800) 533-0331

Zeos International Ltd. (800) 423-5891

iest way to do that is to phone the companies on their toll-free lines to request literature about their products. See the accompanying list for those phone numbers.

In the endless flow of applications software are thousands of programs, with dozens of new ones showing up every week. In addition to the few I've been able to touch on, you'll find catalogs crammed with software and computer magazines full of software ads. You can pick from hundreds of shareware programs available for a few dollars a disk and can even download free software from on-line services.

Sources for everything mentioned in this chapter appear either in the accompanying list of computer companies or at the end of this book in the Source Directory. Browse through the directory, and phone or write for catalogs.

CHAPTER NINE

MANAGING YOUR PHOTOGRAPHY BUSINESS

J ust as there are different photographic styles and innumerable ways to compose, light, and shoot any subject, so too do management styles vary greatly. Moreover, what works for one manager may not work for the next. Successful management styles are based on sound business principles, experieince, good sense, and innate intelligence.

Plenty of books and articles are available on various facets of business operation, particularly those of small-business management. Not all the publications are good ones, though, and not all the good ones are equally useful or applicable to your business.

You can't learn everything you need to know about managing from books, or even from a four-year college program in business administration. You must also learn from experience, which—pardon my nagging— is another reason for starting your home-based photography business on a part-time basis. Moreover, you should possess certain attributes that are even more important than education and experience.

You can manage a business without formal schooling in business management. You can manage a business without prior management experience. You cannot expect to succeed, however, without common sense and the capacity to think and reason. An indecisive person who has trouble solving problems can forget about starting a home-based business.

SETTING GOALS

We're often told, sometimes preached at, that as business managers we must set goals, both short-term and long-term. Well, of course we must. Common sense tells us that no one could expect to run a successful operation without knowing what to do tomorrow, or next week, or three months from now. Continued success depends on knowing what to do next year and the year after. That, simply, is what goal setting is all about. Chances are, you're already involved in the process in a big way. If you are planning to open your own home-based photography business, you have set a major goal. If you're working on a business plan, you're engaged in both short-term and long-term goal setting.

Setting goals is a fairly simple procedure, not unlike taking an automobile trip. First, determine your destination. Second, pick the best route. Third, pay attention to your progress along the way. Fourth, keep glancing in your rear-view mirror so you'll know what's coming up behind you. Fifth, watch out for the other guy. Sixth, try to stay ahead of schedule without getting in trouble.

Some people recommend setting goals that are easy to accomplish, but I think this is a mistake, especially for the home-based entrepreneur. You should set goals that make you hustle and keep you from succumbing to all the temptations and distractions around the house. In short, set reasonable goals—difficult to reach but not unattainable.

JOB PLANNING, FORECASTING, AND SCHEDULING

In Chapter 4 you learned that the operation of your business amounts, in large part, to the management of money and the management of time. If you properly manage money and time, your business will probably succeed. But that's like saying, if you master light and lighting, you'll probably be a successful photographer. The job isn't quite so simple as it sounds, yet it needn't be the cumbersome exercise many make of it.

Managing Time

Time management is a matter of knowing all you have to do and how much time you have to accomplish it, then assigning priorities to most tasks and creating a schedule that allows you to get everything done.

Everything. You can't get by with managing only your business time; you must manage all your time to make room for the many jobs, chores, and attendant details in your busy life.

Making Lists

If you're not a list maker, become one. To a greater extent than you might realize, running a business mainly amounts to creating, organizing, and using lists.

1. Every
2. good
3. manager
4. I've
5. known
6. was
7. a
8. list
9. maker
10. .

When making any long-range list of projects and chores, don't dawdle over details. Just empty your mind on paper, minus the minutiae. Assign priorities and see to scheduling later. Begin with the wide-angle view, and gradually focus on the close-up details.

Scheduling Work

In my business I schedule work annually, quarterly, monthly, weekly, and daily. During the last quarter of a year, I usually begin working in my spare time, at a comfortable pace, preparing a schedule for the coming year. As December bears down on me, I pick up the pace so I can finish the annual schedule before Christmas. Then between Christmas and New Year's, I create my first-quarter and January schedules.

I routinely do my quarterly scheduling at the end of December, March, June, and September and monthly scheduling on the last day or two of the preceding month. My workweek runs Monday through Sunday, so I see to weekly scheduling on Sunday evenings. I take care of daily scheduling every evening. That way, I've already planned my workday by the time I get up in the morning.

I lay out my annual schedule by listing, broadly and generally, everything I intend to accomplish during the coming year. This schedule takes the form of several lists where I group like items: Business Chores, Business Maintenance, Business Correspondence, Capital Investment, and Shopping (photography and office materials and supplies). I also account for demands on my personal time by making similar lists: Personal Chores, House Maintenance, Major Projects, Personal Correspondence, Major Purchases, and Shopping.

Not all aspects of my business end up on lists. Many I just note on my calendar so I can keep track and take action as necessary. Some are so obvious by now that I don't bother listing them or noting them anywhere. For example, I no longer need to remind myself that my big insurance bills come due in June and December, or that the Sheriff of Nottingham will tie his noble steed to my hitching post in November when he comes collecting m'lord's property taxes, or that April 15 is a day that will forever live in infamy in the minds of all Americans. These things I know.

Setting Priorities

My quarterly lists grow out of my annual list, the monthly schedules out of the quarterly ones, and so on. My annual schedule is broad and general, and I assign no priorities to the items on it, other than flagging certain jobs I want to get done in a particular quarter or month. Even my quarterly schedules are fairly free of priority assignments.

My monthly schedule usually contains (1) all the chores, jobs, and projects that *must* be done that month; (2) some that I want to finish that month, if possible; and (3) a few that I'll get to if time permits, but it's no big deal if I don't. Although I don't actually number the items on my schedule, those are the three priorities I work with.

Business Planners and Calendars

In an effort to keep track of all this, I have tried perhaps a dozen different sizes and styles of planners but have never been wholly satisfied with any. I've used pocket-size and desk-size planning systems from a variety of publishers. For a couple of years, I used a Cambridge planner, consisting of a 7-by-9-inch three-ring binder with assorted calendars and dividers. I customized it to fit my business needs by adding a set of alphabetical index-tab dividers that enabled me to turn quickly to lists, schedules, and notes. For some reason, though, when I was ready to order refills, Quill had stopped carrying Cambridge products, and I couldn't find what I needed locally. Fortunately, a good friend and colleague gave me a Franklin Quest planner/calendar for Christmas, and it proved outstanding in most respects.

You probably won't find a planner/calendar that's perfect for you and your business in every way. The secret to making a planner/calendar work well is to customize it to fit your specific needs.

The only advice I can offer you is to consider your needs and go shopping. You'll find planners and systems of every shape, size, and purpose at office-supply outlets, many department stores, and some mail-order sources. There is even planner/calendar software available for those who are never far from their computers or carry laptop or notebook computers with them. You'll also find software that works in conjunction with conventional planners.

Some people like to keep a separate business diary; I don't. My planner/calendar is a record of most of my business dealings and transactions, assignments, meetings, phone calls, correspondence, and more. I see no reason to duplicate any of this. Consequently, I do not discard my various to-do lists and schedules. Instead, I save and file them as a record of my business. I suggest you do likewise, or keep a business diary if you prefer.

When you eventually grow weary of searching for the perfect planner, while using the inferior or inappropriate designs of others, perhaps you'll do as I did not long ago and create your own.

I used my computer to design standard 8½-by-11 inch planner pages, then ran them through a three-hole punch so they would fit in a large, zippered ring binder that keeps everything handy and organized. As I use up a month's worth of pages, I file them in a standard 1-inch (ring size) binder that holds a year's worth of documents as a permanent record of my business activities.

I have planner pages for listing and scheduling business and other activities by the day, week, month, and quarter, which I'll share with you (see pages 214–221). You can use them as they are, or as idea sources for designing pages that better accommodate your business and personal life.

You'll notice that I have three different designs for the daily planner pages. The first one is for the busiest of people who need a full page per day to keep track of all they must do (see page 155). I assigned this one the eight-element DOS file name "DAYAWFUL."

The person whose business day is merely hectic and complex might prefer the set with the file name "DAYCMPLX," which requires four pages per week. The format is identical for the Monday/Tuesday, Wednesday/Thursday, and Friday/Saturday pages (see page 156). The left column of the fourth page lays out Sunday the same as other days, but the right column provides space for journal entries and reminders for the coming week (see page 157).

The simplest day planner is "DAYSIMPL." This one lays out the entire week in two pages, with room left on the second page for journal entries and reminders (see page 158–159). While this may be the simplest of all three designs, it is deceptively so. This is not a planner for people who don't have much to do; it's the one for people who have plenty to do but have their lives under control.

If you need the page-a-day planner, as I once did, I suggest you spend time examining your business to find ways to streamline it. The idea here is to eventually get your life organized enough for you to use the two-page-a-day planner. Then keep working at it until the simple four-page-a-day version is all you need. I've reached a point where I'm actually leaving some lines blank most days.

The daily planner is for getting down to specifics; the weekly planner can be a bit more general. Nevertheless, it shows some specific items—such as appointments, meetings, and correspondence—that just get transferred to the daily planner in a timely fashion (see page 160).

The monthly planner is broader yet. It requires one page per month, and each page is identical to the others (see page 161).

Quarterly planners are for listing and scheduling the major projects and keeping track of the more distant deadlines and income due. The four pages required are identical, except for the month names (see page 162).

Keep watch for ways to customize these pages to suit your needs. On the daily planner pages, for example, you might want to dedicate some space to certain activities you repeat daily or regularly. If you walk, run, or ride a bike for fitness, you might wish to record your daily mileage. Perhaps you're dieting and want to count calories. Or you might want to keep track of the time you spend working out on exercise equipment.

MONDAY: _____ / _____

Appointments/Meetings:

1. _____
2. _____
3. _____
4. _____
5. _____

Must Do (Priority 1):

1. _____
2. _____
3. _____
4. _____
5. _____
6. _____
7. _____
8. _____
9. _____
10. _____

Should Do (Priority 2):

1. _____
2. _____
3. _____
4. _____
5. _____
6. _____
7. _____
8. _____
9. _____
10. _____

Try To Do (Priority 3):

1. _____
2. _____
3. _____
4. _____
5. _____
6. _____
7. _____
8. _____

Phone/E-mail/Letters:

1. _____
2. _____
3. _____
4. _____
5. _____
6. _____
7. _____
8. _____
9. _____
10. _____

Notes/Reminders:

_____
_____
_____
_____
_____
_____
_____
_____
_____
_____
_____
_____

Journal:

_____
_____
_____
_____
_____
_____
_____
_____
_____
_____
_____
_____
_____

MONDAY: _____ / _____

Notes: _____

_____

_____

_____

_____

Appointments/Meetings:

_____

_____

_____

_____

_____

Phone/E-mail/Correspondence:

_____

_____

_____

_____

_____

_____

_____

_____

_____

Must Do Today (Priority 1):

_____

_____

_____

_____

_____

_____

_____

_____

Should Do Today (Priority 2):

_____

_____

_____

_____

TUESDAY: _____ / _____

Notes: _____

_____

_____

_____

_____

Appointments/Meetings:

_____

_____

_____

_____

_____

Phone/E-mail/Correspondence:

_____

_____

_____

_____

_____

_____

_____

_____

_____

Must Do Today (Priority 1):

_____

_____

_____

_____

_____

_____

_____

_____

Should Do Today (Priority 2):

_____

_____

_____

_____

SUNDAY: _____ / _____

JOURNAL

Notes: _____

_____

_____

_____

_____

_____

Appointments/Meetings:

_____

_____

_____

_____

_____

Phone/E-mail/Correspondence:

_____

_____

_____

_____

_____

_____

_____

_____

Must Do Today (Priority 1):

_____

_____

_____

_____

_____

_____

_____

_____

Should Do Today (Priority 2):

_____

_____

_____

_____

_____

Next Week:

MONDAY: _____ / _____

Notes: _____
_____
_____
_____
_____

To Do Today:

1. _____
2. _____
3. _____
4. _____
5. _____
6. _____
7. _____
8. _____
9. _____
10. _____
11. _____
12. _____

TUESDAY: _____ / _____

Notes: _____
_____
_____
_____
_____

To Do Today:

1. _____
2. _____
3. _____
4. _____
5. _____
6. _____
7. _____
8. _____
9. _____
10. _____
11. _____
12. _____

WEDNESDAY: _____ / _____

Notes: _____
_____
_____
_____
_____

To Do Today:

1. _____
2. _____
3. _____
4. _____
5. _____
6. _____
7. _____
8. _____
9. _____
10. _____
11. _____
12. _____

THURSDAY: _____ / _____

Notes: _____
_____
_____
_____
_____

To Do Today:

1. _____
2. _____
3. _____
4. _____
5. _____
6. _____
7. _____
8. _____
9. _____
10. _____
11. _____
12. _____

FRIDAY: _____ / _____

Notes: _____
_____
_____
_____
_____

To Do Today:
1. _____
2. _____
3. _____
4. _____
5. _____
6. _____
7. _____
8. _____
9. _____
10. _____
11. _____
12. _____

SATURDAY: _____ / _____

Notes: _____
_____
_____
_____
_____

To Do Today:
1. _____
2. _____
3. _____
4. _____
5. _____
6. _____
7. _____
8. _____
9. _____
10. _____
11. _____
12. _____

SUNDAY: _____ / _____

Notes: _____
_____
_____
_____
_____

To Do Today:
1. _____
2. _____
3. _____
4. _____
5. _____
6. _____
7. _____
8. _____
9. _____
10. _____
11. _____
12. _____

JOURNAL

_____
_____
_____
_____
_____
_____
_____
_____
_____
_____
_____

Next Week:

_____
_____
_____
_____
_____
_____
_____

WEEK: _____ / _____

Appointments/Meetings:

_____
_____
_____
_____
_____
_____

Notes/Reminders:

_____
_____
_____
_____
_____
_____

Photography:

1. _____
2. _____
3. _____
4. _____
5. _____
6. _____
7. _____
8. _____
9. _____
10. _____
11. _____
12. _____
13. _____
14. _____
15. _____
16. _____
17. _____
18. _____
19. _____
20. _____

Phone/E-mail/Letters:

1. _____
2. _____
3. _____
4. _____
5. _____
6. _____
7. _____
8. _____
9. _____
10. _____
11. _____
12. _____
13. _____
14. _____
15. _____

Chores:

1. _____
2. _____
3. _____
4. _____
5. _____
6. _____
7. _____
8. _____
9. _____
10. _____
11. _____
12. _____
13. _____
14. _____
15. _____

Top Prority/Must Do:

1. _____
2. _____
3. _____
4. _____
5. _____
6. _____
7. _____
8. _____
9. _____
10. _____

Appointments/Meetings:

Top Priority/Must Do:

Photography:

Business/Household Chores:

January Projects:

_____
_____
_____
_____
_____
_____
_____
_____
_____
_____
_____
_____

February Projects:

_____
_____
_____
_____
_____
_____
_____
_____
_____
_____
_____
_____

March Projects:

_____
_____
_____
_____
_____
_____
_____
_____
_____
_____
_____
_____

Household Projects:

_____
_____
_____
_____
_____
_____
_____
_____
_____
_____
_____
_____

Deadlines:

_____
_____
_____
_____
_____
_____
_____

Royalties Due:

_____
_____
_____
_____
_____
_____
_____

Design other pages to further specialize and customize your planner. You can also add alphabetical, monthly, and other index tabs; page finders; printed calendars; plastic pocket pages; business-card holders; and other items you'll find in the Quill catalog and at local office-supply outlets.

STORAGE, FILING, AND RETRIEVAL SYSTEMS

Every business in America is confronted with the management of a tremendous amount of paperwork that gets more unwieldy every year. Most managers must also find convenient ways to store directories, manuals, and reference books of all kinds. As a professional photographer, you will also need to create efficient and safe storage and retrieval systems for the thousands of negatives, transparencies, and prints your business will generate.

As a self-employed photographer, you will be able to exercise some control over the paperwork snarl, but don't expect total success. To give you an idea of how severe the problem is, my local post office receives eight bags of mail for every bag it sends out, which means that on the average, postal patrons in my community get eight times as much mail as they generate. In my case, the ratio is even more lopsided—probably about twenty pounds received for every pound I send out.

If, like many aspiring entrepreneurs, you haven't given much thought to managing this paper mountain, you had better do so immediately. The best time to set up the system you will need is now. If you wait until paperwork is stacked in teetering piles or until you have a closetful of little yellow boxes of slides, sorting and filing will be worse chores than they already are.

THE REFERENCE LIBRARY

If you aren't buying books and subscribing to magazines on photography, you're not keeping up with what has become one of the most rapidly changing technologies in the world. Continuing education is part of the business; you must read and study to remain competitive. Unless you have a photographic memory (no pun intended) you will need to set up a reference library consisting of bookshelves and filing cabinets.

Books and Directories

Your library must have the capacity to house not only your photographic books but also volumes relating to your photographic specialties and other aspects of your business. Allow for plenty of shelf space, and keep in mind that your library will continue to grow for as long as you're in business.

When you're setting up your work space, plan to use any available empty walls for bookshelves. In the beginning you might be able to get by with one or two small bookcases, but eventually you will need something more capacious. Floor-to-ceiling shelves represent the most efficient use of wall space and can be inexpensive and easy to install.

If you're looking to cut costs, which should be foremost in the mind of any entrepreneur, plan to install shelving yourself. If you're handy around the house or know anything about woodworking, you already know how to build bookshelves. Putting up shelves requires only the simplest tools and basic techniques, so don't be intimidated by the idea of doing a little carpentry.

Various lumber and wood products work well as shelving. The most common are fir, pine, cedar, and other softwood 1-by-10 lumber, usually available in lengths of 8, 10, 12, 14, 16, and 20 feet.

Plywood also makes good shelving. It comes in 4-by-8-foot sheets and sometimes smaller pieces, in various thicknesses. The ideal for shelves is ¾-inch-thick plywood. You can cut it into shelf-wide lengths, or have it cut for you at a lumberyard.

Particle board also comes in 4-by-8-foot sheets and in shelving dimensions and various thicknesses. The ¾-inch stock is the best for shelves.

To keep shelves from sagging under the weight of heavy books, wood and plywood shelves should be supported at least every 36 inches, or better yet, every 30 inches. Supports for the weaker particle-board shelves should be no more than 30, and ideally only 24, inches apart.

Stop by a public library, bookstore, or department store to find woodworking books containing ideas and designs for shelving. Then browse through home-improvement centers to learn what's available in the way of shelving brackets, fixtures, and other hardware.

I started amassing my library when I was a teenager, and I continue adding books to it every year. With more than 3,000 volumes, my library takes up shelf space in our master bedroom, guest room, and living room, as well as throughout my work complex. In my darkroom I have 3-foot-long shelves, floor to ceiling, holding my photography books, darkroom manuals, and darkroom supplies. My office shelf unit is twice as long, and also 8 feet high. Bookshelves run along 15 feet of walls in my studio. In my work complex alone are 192 square feet of bookshelves.

Research Files

Another indispensable part of my reference library is my research files, which also continue to grow, sometimes at alarming rates. Counting two-drawer and four-drawer filing cabinets and desks with file drawers, I have thirty drawers full of business and research files on various subjects and will be adding at least two more four-drawer cabinets within the next few months.

I go through the file drawers every couple of years to discard outdated material and route inactive files to dead storage. When I reach a point where all drawers are full of active files and I can't make more room, I have no alternative but to add more drawers to the system.

You might be wondering why the sole proprietor of a small home-based business would need so much bookshelf and file-drawer space. Although I buy some books and subscribe to a couple of magazines for simple enjoyment, most of the books and file materials just accumulate as part of my business and as a result of both short-term and long-term projects I get involved in.

For example, much of my work is outdoor and travel photography and writing, and the area I cover is the Pacific Coast. In working that beat, I like to have a good background in the history, geology, climate, and wildlife of the region. Consequently, over the years, I have gathered well over a hundred books about California, Oregon, Washington, British Columbia, and Alaska. I also have eight file drawers full of articles, notes, and other research materials covering the same region. Two shelves in my studio hold the phone directories of all the coastal communities of California, Oregon, and Washington.

During the past two years, I've concentrated my work on the inter-tidal areas—estuaries, salt marshes, tide flats, rocky shores, and beaches—and the wildlife that abounds in these places. In that time, I have crammed two large file drawers to overflowing and have filled a shelf with fifty-two books and book-length reports on coastal ecosystems, marine biology, natural history, and related topics.

So in addition to the substantial normal flow of paper through my office are the topical floods that often strain my dikes and levies and threaten to overflow. Containing the torrents is just a lot of dam work.

BUSINESS FILES

Perhaps a better analogy would be to think of all this business paperwork as a vast and disorderly herd of cattle, with just enough wild and rangy long-horns mixed in to create the potential for stampedes. As range boss, your job is to keep this unruly bunch of critters headed in the right direction.

The idea is to eventually get every piece of essential paper into its proper place—a file where similar papers are kept. What's most frustrating, though, is that the paperwork you deal with is a mass of miscellany. Directing each piece from a general pile into a specific file is among the most tedious of tasks. The process can be streamlined and vastly improved.

An Efficient Interim Filing System

Set up an interim file system that will corral groups of related documents. Use the same principle to move paper through your entire business process until it eventually ends up in neatly and conveniently stored file folders.

In the good old days, before we wasted so much paper, a typical business manager was able to maintain reasonable control with the aid of the cubbyholes in a roll-top desk and three file trays. The life of the business manager, however, has become far too complicated to be organized with three baskets labeled *In, Out,* and *Pending.*

You'll find a number of products available for performing these yeoman duties, such as desktop sorters and organizers, literature sorters, and all kinds of stacking trays and baskets.

Commercially available desktop organizers come in metal or wood and are freestanding units that can add the efficiency of the old roll-top desk to any modern desk or worktable. They come in various sizes and capacities, but all are limited in their usefulness to mainly keeping desktops uncluttered.

Literature organizers resemble bookcases with numerous cubbyholes designed for routing and holding standard letter-size documents. They're usually made of metal, corrugated board, or both. Some are modular stacking units that you can add to as your needs dictate. You'll find them available in sizes ranging from six to seventy-two compartments.

One stacking tray or basket will hold about as much paperwork as one compartment of a literature organizer. A system of trays probably costs slightly more than a literature organizer of comparable capacity, but trays have the advantage of versatility; they fit practically anywhere, and the system easily expands by one or a dozen units at a time.

When my home-based business was a part-time venture, I got by fine with a system consisting of a dozen trays. As my business has grown and expanded into many areas, the system has had to grow with it and now consists of seventy-six trays.

I'm not going to list all the subject labels, but I will tell you how I've labeled some of these trays to keep paper organized and moving. Standing in my office between a four-drawer filing cabinet and bookshelves is a stack of seventeen trays that handle all my highest-priority paperwork and most of what accumulates in my daily mail. Among them are trays labeled *Priority 1,* for anything requiring action within seven days, and *Priority 2,* for action within thirty days. Seven trays are for specifically routed correspondence, and one is labeled *Miscellaneous Correspondence.* The *Order* tray holds paperwork for products, literature, and anything else I need to order during the month. The tray labeled *File* is for anything I've acted on that is now ready for routing to a specific file tray and ultimately to a folder in a filing cabinet. The top tray in the stack holds my outgoing mail until my next trip to the post office.

Despite the tonnage of catalogs you receive regularly, I'll bet you can never find the one you're looking for. Murphy must have a law about that. Solve your problem, as I did, with stacking trays. I have five on a bookshelf in my studio, labeled *Outdoor, Home/Shop, Office, Photography,* and *Miscellaneous.* Catalogs I keep go into the appropriate trays and regularly get replaced with new ones.

The remaining trays in my interim system are also in my studio, stacked atop my four-drawer filing cabinets. Some are highly active, fill up fast, and require regular maintenance. Others lead quieter existences.

Among the most active are my follow-up files for proposals, queries, film, photographs, and manuscripts. Other busy files include *Accounts Payable, Accounts Receivable,* and *Business Taxes.*

To give you an idea of how preliminary routing works for my research files, here's how some of my other stacking trays are labeled: *Travel, Maps, General Outdoors, Boating/Canoeing, Insects, Plants, Environment/Conservation, Estuaries/Wetlands, Oceans/Seas, Fish/Shellfish, Birds/Waterfowl, Mammals/Marsupials,* and *Reptiles/Amphibians.* With trays so labeled, in mere minutes I'm able to turn a big stack of miscellaneous paperwork into presorted groups that make the final filing job much easier.

I also have four trays labeled *Photography, Slides, Negatives,* and *Prints.* Magazine articles, instruction sheets, and other documents related to photography go into the *Photography* tray to await further sorting and later filing in my filing cabinets. In the other three trays are slides, negatives with contact sheets, and prints waiting to be filed or refiled.

I make my tray labels with self-adhesive plastic embossing tape and one of those little Dymo label makers. If you use plastic stacking trays, you may find that embossed-tape labels don't stick as well as they should and eventually come off. Here's a tip. Wrap a cloth or paper towel around your finger, dampen it with cigarette-lighter fluid, and wipe the surface where you plan to affix the label. By the time you peel the backing off the label, the surface will be dry and ready, and the label will stay stuck. If you ever need to change a label on a tray, lighter fluid will also remove any gummy residue left by the old label.

An interim filing system is easy to maintain and serves several valuable purposes. First, it lets you sort and route paperwork quickly and efficiently. When you need something that has not yet made it to a file folder, it's far easier to sort through the paperwork in one file tray than to paw through stacks of miscellaneous magazines, articles, catalogs, and other accumulated paperwork, in the process wasting untold amounts of time.

By far, the greatest value of my interim system is that it keeps me from being buried in paperwork while allowing me to put off the actual job of filing until the absolute last second.

An Active Filing System

I have also worked to make my active files easier to use and maintain. Over a period of about two years, I gradually converted all my file drawers to hanging files. If you're not familiar with them, hanging-file systems consist of inexpensive metal racks from which specially made folders are suspended.

The racks are easy to assemble and install in any filing cabinet or desk file drawer. In my system I use standard and box-bottom (large-capacity) hanging folders to hold all the materials I keep in manila file folders. The advantage to a hanging system is that file folders stand upright and are easily removed and returned without other folders falling over.

During recent years I have also color-coded many of my active files with self-adhesive file-folder labels. That makes it a lot easier to locate a particular file folder in any stack of folders I'm currently working with. Every folder in my Oregon files, for example, has a folder-tab label with a narrow red stripe across the top. Washington files are green, California brown, and estuary files black.

You'll find such labels available in perhaps two dozen colors at most office-supply outlets. Colored file folders offer another way to color-code your filing system.

Computer Files

Computers offer users a convenient way to reduce much of the paperwork shuffling by filing material electronically. Although I doubt that computer storage will ever be able to entirely replace conventional filing systems, it can help streamline the filing process and certainly promises even greater use and versatility in the future.

What I have stored on diskettes in two small cabinets would probably fill several four-drawer filing cabinets and many feet of bookshelves.

Dead Files

Filing cabinets are expensive. Corrugated filing boxes are cheap. Use filing cabinets for all your important active files. Use the corrugated filing boxes for dead files—those that aren't active but must be retained for one reason or another. Tax files for previous years, for example, can go into a dead file instead of taking up valuable space in a cabinet. You'll no doubt find other files you must keep but don't use very often that would be better routed to a dead file.

Quill Corporation and other office suppliers sell boxes for this purpose. As you fill each box, label it clearly with a felt marker, and store it in any dry storage area. Although you can box up any kind of paperwork for dead storage, don't store photographic material this way. Negatives, contact sheets, transparencies, and prints require special handling and filing.

PHOTOGRAPHIC FILING SYSTEMS

Filing photographic materials is never as exciting as the picture-taking process or as rewarding as creative darkroom work, but it needn't be the oppressively monotonous labor so many make of it. Moreover, it's essential for serious photographers.

Over the years, I have used several photographic filing systems, all of which failed in some way. I followed the advice of others and became mired in complex indexing systems. When I chucked indexing altogether and simply filed everything in cabinets by subject, it worked wonderfully for a few months, but the absence of an index led to retrieval problems that compounded with time. I've concluded that indexing is necessary for consistency, rapid retrieval, and speedy and accurate refiling, but it can be carried to time-consuming extremes.

One professional I know of, for example, has incorporated the Dewey Decimal System into his slide filing and is actually pleased about it. He assigns *every slide* a file number, which he transcribes onto two file sheets: one describing the subject in detail, another listing such data as an eight-digit call number, five-digit location code, date filed, date taken, and something called "other." Then he enters a complete description and history on a 3-by-5-inch index card, which also gets filed. It boggles the mind!

Simplicity Is the Key to Filing Success

To my way of thinking, basic simplicity, logic and memory tie-in, minimal duplication of information, ease of maintenance, low cost of operation, rapid retrieval, and safe storage are elementary for any photographic filing system.

Simplicity saves time and is an incentive to users for keeping files current. Complicated filing tasks are sheer drudgery, too easily put off.

Inasmuch as we all learned numerical progression and alphabetical order as children, I see no reason to confound these systems with elaborate codes or needless prefixes that don't tie in to what we already know. There's a simple logic to A-B-C or 1-2-3 progressions. Whereas there may be a logic to indexing symbols that read like credit-card numbers, it's by no means simple. Moreover, such hieroglyphics require deciphering and are barriers to speed and efficiency.

Typical of the system the Dewey Decimal chap uses are numbers such as 599.744 46 T/2716. Have you the remotest idea what those fifteen characters mean? Such a number intimidates me. I get retroactive writer's cramp just thinking about numbering *every one* of my thousands of slides this way. On the other hand, you know as well as I that 472 follows 471, and that M comes before N. Logic tells us that we'll find something numbered 429B beyond something labeled 236A. Consequently, you could go to my files and locate any negative or slide in the same seconds it takes me. What's more, if I hired someone to help me, I could teach my system to the person in under five minutes.

Whether or not a single picture can be worth 10,000 words, the time-worn proverb has merit. Every image contains valuable information that's there for the looking. Furthermore, frame margins provide useful data that needn't be transcribed onto file documents, unless you enjoy work for work's sake.

In any photographic filing and indexing system, question every word, letter, or digit you write down. It may seem niggling to point out that fifteen-element index numbers consume more time than five-element numbers, but consider labeling 1,000 slides and file documents. If the task would take three hours with the shorter number, the fifteen-element system would require nine. Net waste: six hours.

Some photographers incorporate dates into their index numbers, but I decided not to. If the date is important, and often it's not, it will appear in the log I keep when I'm traveling or testing films and equipment. Furthermore, the lab dates all my transparencies. So why duplicate the information?

For similar reasons, I don't record frame numbers, film types, equipment used, shutter and aperture settings, or anything that's available elsewhere. Negative margins show film type and frame number; slide mounts tell me whether I shot Kodachrome or Fujichrome.

Inexpensive, Effective Archival Storage

In my system I wanted maximum protection for minimum investment, without sacrificing efficiency. I settled on loose-leaf binders that house negatives and transparencies in archivally safe, transparent plastic pages. They store neatly on a shelf or in metal filing-cabinet drawers, and the system is the least expensive of those I've investigated.

One-inch (ring size) binders are normally available from Quill Corporation (see address at the back of this book, under "Business Equipment and Supplies") for unbelievably low prices and frequently go on sale for even less. Best prices are for lots of one or two dozen.

Plastic storage pages are available from various companies. Many are similar or nearly identical, so look for the best prices and features. Print File is one brand I have used and can recommend. The company offers pages for 35mm and 120 film, as well as 35mm slides. Century Plastics also offers suitable products. For the past several years, I have been using Vue-All products, because the price has been right. Neg-Savers, #8020, hold seven negative strips of five frames each, so I make it a point to start every roll of negative film at the second frame, for a total of thirty-five exposures per roll instead of thirty-six. Slide-Savers, #7060, are top-loaded pages that hold twenty mounted 35mm slides each.

These clear polypropylene pages protect the contents from smudges, dust, and fingerprints. They allow slides to be viewed and negatives to be contact-printed without removal.

Avoid any plastic pages containing polyvinyl chloride (PVC) or harmful plasticizers, which can damage film and transparencies stored in them. Rigid plastic and cardboard open-frame pages will work, but they are more expensive, their bulk reduces binder capacity, and they aren't as dustproof and smudgeproof as polypropylene pages.

It's best to store binders in metal cabinets where they're protected from dust and where you can also enclose bags of chemical desiccant to absorb atmospheric moisture. Some glues in wood cabinets, and even the wood itself, if not properly sealed, can be harmful to photographic materials.

Efficient Indexing, Filing, and Retrieval Systems

If you decide to use my system for indexing and filing negatives and contact sheets, you'll need a supply of 3-by-5 index cards, alphabetical index tabs, an index-card box or cabinet, and a three-hole paper punch.

I store negatives in simple numerical order, fifty contact sheets and negative pages per binder. I subdivide each binder with five loose-leaf index-tab pages that lead instantly to any group of ten contact sheets. I assign a number to every negative set and corresponding contact sheet. The first one in my first binder is simply labeled #1.

I enter contact-sheet numbers on 3-by-5 cards that I store alphabetically by subject and cross-reference as required. If I devote an entire roll of film to one subject, that number will appear on a single card in the file, unless I want to cross-reference it. When several subjects appear on any contact sheet, I enter the number on appropriate cards. As I accumulate more negatives of subjects on file, I add the new numbers to the cards in columns beneath the subjects written at the top.

I also file transparencies in numerical order, with twenty-five pages (500 slides) to a binder. Inasmuch as each slide gets numbered, though, I modified the system to keep numbers short. The first 1,000 slides are numbered 000 through 999. The next 1,000 are numbered 000A through 999A, then 000B through 999B, and so on. Consequently, I can file 27,000 slides with index numbers no longer than four characters. Beyond that, a double-letter suffix—AA to AZ, BA to BZ, and on to ZZ—permits filing up to 703,000 (gulp!) slides with numbers only five characters long.

ALASKA				
18	178	192	206	224
24	179	193	207	225
33	180	194	208	226
150	181	195	209	227
161	182	196	211	228
162	183	197	212	229
170	184	198	216	230
171	185	199	217	231
172	186	200	218	232
173	187	201	219	234
174	188	202	220	235
175	189	203	221	238
176	190	204	222	239
177	191	205	223	259

Index Card for Negative File

TRANSPARENCY FILE

Subject _____

FILE NO.	IDENTIFICATION	DATE	NOTES & CROSS-REFERENCES

For transparencies, I made a letter-size file sheet with a typewriter, had it offset printed at a quick-print shop, then hole-punched the pages for binders organized with alphabetical index tabs. Pages are labeled according to subject, and each has a capacity for twenty-five slides and appropriate information.

Most important is to assign a number to every page of negatives and every transparency; then it's retrievable. You can further refine the system by cross-referencing, which merely lists numbers under two or more subject headings as a convenience. Cross-reference only if it will facilitate access; otherwise, it will be an unnecessary burden.

Subjects that don't seem to fit anywhere are natural candidates for the "Miscellaneous" file. Some find this a great catch-all category, but remember, if you file everything under "Miscellaneous," you have no filing system at all.

In addition to "Miscellaneous" negative cards and transparency sheets, I have a card and page under each letter of the alphabet for respective miscellany: "A—Miscellaneous," "B—Miscellaneous," and so on. These are handy for listing subjects I may or may not ever photograph again.

I sometimes need to upgrade the miscellaneous shots, though. For instance, I might file a single shot of a fire engine under "F—Miscellaneous." If I amass other fire-engine photos, I then start a card or sheet labeled "Fire Engines" and transfer the numbers to the new file.

I also label the binder spines and stand the binders spine up in my filing-cabinet drawers. The first binder in my negative files is labeled *Contacts & Negatives #1 to #50*; the next, *Contacts & Negatives #51 to #100*; and so on. The first binder in my transparency files is labeled *Transparencies #000 to #499*; the next, *Transparencies #500 to #999*; then, *Transparencies #000A to #499A*; and so on.

I began storing my transparency file sheets in a binder labeled *Transparency Master File*, which I subdivided with alphabetical index-tab pages. As that binder filled, I had to divide the master file in two and store it in two binders: *Volume I—A to L* and *Volume II—M to Z*. These binders are now filling, and I will soon have to add another binder or two to the master file.

It's a remarkably simple and efficient system that enables me to find any negative or transparency in minutes. In fact, you could find any photograph of mine just as fast, having never seen my system before.

Let's say you and I are collaborating on a project, a brochure for a tour-bus company that plans to run guided tours in northern California. Among the photographs the client wants is a good color shot of the historic Carson Mansion in Eureka. You pull the *Transparency Master File—Volume I*, turn to the E section, find the file sheets titled "Eureka, California," run your finger down the first column, and find that transparencies 645B through 651B are of the Carson Mansion.

From the same drawer that holds the master-file binders, you pull a binder titled *Transparencies 500B to 999B* and turn immediately to the page containing transparencies 640B to 659B. And there they are—seven shots of the mansion under sunny skies.

For most of us, filing is never enjoyable, but the greatest drudgery is often self-imposed and needless. There are some sophisticated systems that allow users to locate in seconds what might take me a minute or two to find. But such systems require many more hours of setup and maintenance than I spend—hours and days I prefer to use traipsing along the coast, working with cameras.

(Names and addresses of companies offering image-management software appear in the Source Directory at the back of the book, under the heading "Computer Software and Services." Write or phone these companies, requesting information about their programs.)

PROBLEMS IN MANAGING YOUR BUSINESS

No business runs so perfectly or smoothly that there's never a problem, but the manager who works to anticipate problems is usually able to sidestep them and keep on course with a minimum of hassles and hardships.

Identifying Problems

So what kinds of problems might the home-based photographer face? Every aspect of your business can be a problem. You can have problems with vendors, customers, and other people. Your business vehicle, photography equipment, and office equipment can give you trouble. You can have financial, legal, and operational difficulties. You can have insurance problems, tax troubles, and minor irritations or major worries over book-

keeping, paper shuffling, phone service, time management, film processing, printing, plumbing, electricity, the neighbor's cat, termites, and door-
to-door peddlers.

The potential seems boundless, but the right attitude and strategy
can keep catastrophes contained. Understand that running a business is
mainly a matter of encountering, identifying, and solving problems, big
and small. Most of what we've covered so far in this book has to do with
managing minor problems and avoiding major ones.

Don't Needlessly Complicate Matters

If you can think, you can make decisions. If you can make decisions, you
can solve problems. A problem is any matter, concern, or situation posing
an obstacle or causing some degree of difficulty or perplexity in the carrying out of a task. It's as simple as that. Too many people, however, make
a big deal out of it.

In recent years I've read a number of reports and articles from
business-consulting agencies. I've watched some of these consultants in
action, and I've grown especially wary of business gurus who turn decision-
making and problem-solving processes into complex and convoluted
exercises. If I followed all their silly suggestions, I'd never get anything
done.

There's also a tendency among business consultants and academics
to further complicate otherwise simple processes with highfalutin terminology. With the possible exceptions of sociology and literary criticism,
no other discipline is more encumbered with buzzwords, catchphrases,
jargon, and the invention of terms to define.

It's always best to anticipate problems so you can avoid them or deal
with them comfortably and effectively. Like life, however, business is full of
surprises. If you're smart, you'll take them in stride and learn from them.

I'm frequently reminded of the old medical joke in which the physi-
cian asks the patient what his problem is. The patient raises his arm and
says, "It hurts when I do this." The doctor responds, "Then don't do that."

How many times have I made some foolish move and instantly regret-
ted it? Pardon me while I count. Invariably, I think to myself or even say
out loud, "I won't do that again." Live and learn.

PRODUCTIVITY

Productivity is what your business is all about, so you will have to keep track of it, manage for it, and improve it in any way you can.

Analyzing Productivity

Many businesses, especially the larger ones, use reports to analyze and manage productivity. Although managers often custom-design reports for specific purposes, some of the more generic reports contain information that allows experienced managers to track productivity.

Profit-and-loss (P&L) and cash-flow reports are two you can use to analyze your productivity, but they won't prove valuable until after you've been in business awhile. Your first year, you will be working with P&L and cash-flow projections, which are useless in measuring actual production. Even in your second year, you might not find these reports of great value. It takes some practice and experience to be able to scan the columns and translate the numbers into productivity measurements.

The Production/Sales/Income Report

Meanwhile, you may want to design a report that does a better job for you. For a number of years, I used a document I called a Production/Sales/ Income (PSI) report, which I prepared monthly. This is a simple report, easy to compile. It covers gross sales and income but does not include information about expenses and other costs of doing business. If you are unaccustomed to using P&L and cash-flow reports, however, this is a good alternative you might want to try.

I stopped using these reports for several years and instead relied solely on P&L and cash-flow figures, which provide a more accurate picture of net income and profits. I reasoned that this was not only better information but data available to me anyway, which made the PSI reports seem like busywork. I recently decided to reinstate my PSI reports, however, for the very simple reason that I like them. I'm willing to devote the little time required for the gain derived. PSI reports are good exercise, and they provide a different perspective. The reports tell me when I've done a good job and when I haven't—useful praise and prodding.

In conjunction with this report, I use PSI worksheets I keep in the same binder as my business planner and calendar. These are four loose-leaf pages identified at the top as Production, Sales, Assignments, and Income. Each evening, after work, I log in dates, descriptions, and amounts on the proper worksheets, which I then use on the last day of the month to prepare my PSI report.

On the left side of the report, under the heading Production, I list the title or description of every job completed, market produced for, and date of completion. On the right side of the page, I list the actual or estimated value of each job. I do the same under the headings Sales, Assignments, and Income. I total the amounts for each category and use that information in the summary section at the end of the report.

After I enter the information and figures for the month's income, I run a line across the page and put my summary under it. For example, under the heading June Summary, I list Accounts Receivable as of June 1, June Production, June Sales, June Assignments, June Income, Unsold Material Circulating (photos and manuscripts shipped but not yet sold) as of June 30, Accounts Receivable as of June 30, and Year-to-Date Income as of June 30. A quick glance at my summary lets me know where I stand and where I need to concentrate my efforts.

The information under any heading might be artificially inflated or deflated for one reason or another. For example, in looking back through some of my old reports, I found one for March showing I had landed assignments worth $15,600—two $300 assignments and one for $15,000. What's not shown in the raw data, however, is how that income trickled in during the subsequent months.

Some months, production figures can come out extremely low, even as low as $0.00, but without reflecting actual production. It's a matter of how the game is played. I established the rules, which I work and live by. Although I might spend much or even all of a month working on a major project, or several, if I don't finish by month's end, it doesn't get logged in or credited to that month's production. Figures for some later month, then, will end up being artificially inflated, just as this month's figures were deflated.

Figures for sales and income can fluctuate broadly at times but should be relatively stable over the course of a year. The idea is to work to gradually increase both to a comfortable level that provides you with good income and a schedule you can live with.

To make the system work, you need to set production and income

PRODUCTION/SALES/INCOME REPORT—JUNE

PRODUCTION	Actual Value or Estimated Value
1. Faircrest brochure—6/3	$ 1,200.00
2. School Board posters—6/5	300.00
3. PNW Tug & Barge Annual Report—6/12	1,992.55
4. Victoria, B.C., photo spread, *TravelWest*—6/16	650.00
5. Estuary photo spread, *Coastways*—6/19	500.00
6. "Lovely La Conner," *Leisure Travel*—6/20	1,000.00
JUNE PRODUCTION	**$ 5,642.55**

SALES	
1. Stock sale, *BC Life*—6/4	$ 500.00
2. Dogsled-race photos, *American Adventure*—6/12	350.00
3. *Publication Photography*, Aperture Press—6/19	9,500.00
4. Lighthouse photos, Environmental Calendars—6/26	400.00
5. Waterfalls photos, *Wild Places*—6/30	600.00
JUNE SALES	**$ 11,350.00**

ASSIGNMENTS	
1. "Pristine Prints," *Popular Darkroom*—6/1	$ 500.00
2. Cranberry-harvest photos, *Country Harvest*—6/9	650.00
3. "Oregon Wine Country," *TravelWest*—6/17	750.00
4. "San Juan Summer," *Island Hopping*—6/23	1,200.00
JUNE ASSIGNMENTS	**$ 3,100.00**

INCOME	
1. Royalties, Aperture Press—6/3	$ 4,226.90
2. Royalties, Remington House—6/5	1,541.35
3. Stock sales, Wildstock Agency—6/12	2,225.00
4. Coastal aerial photos, Tourism Division—6/22	400.00
JUNE INCOME	**$ 8,393.25**

JUNE SUMMARY	
Accounts Receivable as of June 1	$ 3,680.80
June Production	5,642.55
June Sales	11,350.00
June Assignments	3,100.00
June Income	8,393.25
Unsold material circulating as of June 30	4,650.00
Accounts Receivable as of June 30	12,405.80
Year-to-Date Income as of June 30	31,861.77

goals at the beginning of the year. Come up with a reasonable monthly figure, and work hard to meet it. As a part-timer, you might establish $1,000 or $1,500 as your monthly PSI goal—more or less, depending on your situation. As a full-timer, you might need to make $3,000 to $4,000 or more each month. When you exceed your PSI monthly goal, it feels good, and you can give yourself a pat on the back. When you fall short of your goal, do the same, but make the pat a kick, and aim a little lower on the torso.

BUSINESS COMMUNICATION

Many small-business operators fail to fully appreciate how important written and oral communication are to every business, no matter its size, product, or service. From the onset, you must be prepared to handle all communication professionally and to document all aspects of your business.

Letterhead and Business Cards

Your first order of business should be to design an attractive letterhead and have stationery, envelopes, and business cards printed. You can design a logo or find suitable clip art you can combine with an attractive typeface. If you're no good at this sort of thing, seek help. Some printers can assist with logo design, but not all are skilled at it. You might want to enlist the aid of a graphic artist to provide original art or work with you to come up with a good design.

Try to make your logo simple, uncluttered, and attractive. If possible, avoid artwork that might date the design. You will use your logo often and become associated with it. For that reason, you shouldn't change it unless absolutely necessary, and then make as few modifications as possible.

When you've come up with a design, you'll have to decide what color paper you want, what quality, color of ink, and type of printing. Use good-quality, twenty-pound or heavier bond paper, and avoid heavily textured surfaces. Go with white or cream or a pleasantly muted shade of gray, beige, blue, or green. Stationery, envelopes, and business cards should be the same color.

Ink color should contrast or coordinate with paper color. Just make sure the ink is dark, the paper light. Some common combinations are black ink on white paper, black on gray, dark brown on cream, dark brown on beige, dark blue on light blue, and dark green on light green. You can also pick two or three contrasting colors of ink, but that will increase your costs.

You'll have a choice between raised and flat printing. Raised type has a sharper, classier look, but it's usually more expensive than flat printing and might not be done locally. If you use a computer with a laser printer, order flat printing for stationery and envelopes. Pick whatever suits you for business cards.

You will probably want to use the logo on your various printed forms, such as invoices, work orders, model releases, and statements. It will cost you extra, but the price shouldn't be prohibitive.

Document Your Transactions

Get into the habit of documenting all your business transactions in some way. This doesn't mean you have to write down everything you do in narrative form, although you sometimes should. Every time you write up a work order or type an invoice, you are documenting a transaction, so keep copies for your files. Also make a copy of every business letter you write; it can be a carbon copy, photocopy, or computer copy.

What about documenting phone calls? You have several options. If you keep a business diary, you can log your phone calls there. Some businesses maintain phone diaries for documenting all telephone communications. As I mentioned earlier, I don't keep a business diary; nor do I keep a phone diary. I let my planner system document my day-to-day operations. When I need to take important notes, I use ruled yellow pads I buy by the dozen; then I date the notes and route them to their proper files. I keep one of these pads near each of my telephones so I can take notes on important conversations. I date and file them as I do other notes.

Why all the documentation? First, it keeps you from relying on what might prove to be an unreliable memory. It helps you get jobs done the way customers want them done. It provides dated references for any necessary follow-up or other action. It also protects you and your business in a variety of ways and can be used as evidence in a court of law.

Be Prompt and Courteous

Promptness is the mark of a professional; courtesy is the mark of a person who is pleasing to deal with. So in all your communications, be prompt and courteous. See to all business correspondence in a timely fashion, and return phone calls within twenty-four hours if possible.

FOLLOW-UP

Follow-up is essential and should be timely, but don't make it any more complicated than it needs to be. I often hear colleagues talk about keeping follow-up logs for all their projects and correspondence. They list everything they send out, the date sent, destination, and other information they deem essential. I don't do any of that, yet I have a follow-up system that will rival any in efficiency. It's part of the interim filing system I wrote about earlier in this chapter.

Everything in my business has a paperwork connection. My invoices and statements are carbonless two-part forms—original to the customer, copy for my files. When I write a query or proposal, I keep a copy for follow-up. When I mail a roll or a batch of transparency film to the lab, I have a mailer stub for follow-up. When I send pictures to an agent or publisher, I submit a caption sheet or caption manuscript, a copy of which I keep for follow-up. When I mail an article or book manuscript, I send a cover letter with it, and—you guessed it—keep a copy for follow-up.

My follow-up file trays are labeled *Proposal Follow-up, Query/Film Follow-up, Manuscript Follow-up, General Follow-up,* and *Accounts Receivable.* The job of follow-up is a simple matter of going to these trays at the end of the month and examining contents for anything that requires attention.

I send a statement to any client who hasn't paid his bill that month. I then attach a copy of the statement to any previous paperwork and return it to the *Accounts Receivable* tray. As I receive letters of acceptance, sales vouchers, and transfer-of-rights agreements, they too go into this tray for follow-up.

When manuscripts and photographs have been out for eight weeks without payment or response, I send follow-up letters, copies of which I attach to the original paperwork and return to the appropriate follow-up tray. I then allow an additional thirty days before sending a more forceful letter, which I then follow up by phone. I note on the most recent paperwork the dates and gist of any phone calls.

Anything that doesn't fit the category of any other follow-up file tray goes into the *General Follow-up* tray.

I don't have to do a tremendous amount of follow-up. In fact, with my receivables it's usually a matter of just pulling all the copies of invoices, statements, and such as they're paid. So there are usually only a few left at the end of a month, and some months there's nothing left in the tray except that month's new billing.

I have considered turning all this over to my computer, but I haven't been able to devise a cost-effective computer billing and follow-up system that's as simple as my manual system.

PROCRASTINATION

As you can see, I put this section off until last. Despite all the words of warning in the various guides for small-business operators and home-based entrepreneurs, procrastination is not the damning malady we're led to believe. Truth be known, I think most of us, by nature, are procrastinators. In fact, I'm not sure I could trust (or believe) anyone who claims to have never procrastinated. The trick is to avoid giving in to the urge too often and to never jeopardize a deadline simply because you don't feel like doing a job.

Few chronic procrastinators ever end up running their own businesses. Anyone who's that bad about putting things off is also apt to put off starting a business.

Anyone with brains enough to get up in the morning knows you can't constantly put jobs off and expect your business to succeed. There will be days when you just don't feel like working or jobs you hate doing. But you'll get the work done anyway, because that's your job, and you're a professional. The success of your business depends on those simple facts.

So, should you worry about procrastination? I think you can put that off for now.

CHAPTER TEN

MARKETING YOUR PHOTOGRAPHY BUSINESS

Marketing is your ultimate business purpose; it means promoting and selling yourself and your services. Marketing encompasses every aspect and activity of your home-based business. All your purposes and efforts should combine to create a process that transfers goods and services to the consumer. First, last, and always, your business *is* marketing.

CREATING A MARKETABLE REPUTATION

The magnitude of the marketing effort surprises many start-up entrepreneurs. It's a big and important job that takes a lot of time and effort, especially in the beginning. Much of it amounts to building a sound and salable reputation, then researching and locating potential clients. During the early stages of your business, all this might consume more than half your time.

When I started my business as a part-timer, I wasn't wholly prepared for the task and how my time would be divided. I was naive enough to think I could spend countless hours traipsing through fields and forests, mountains and meadows, beaches and headlands, recording my experiences with words and pictures. I thought I could devote any time left to the more mundane matters of managing a business and marketing my masterpieces. In short, I saw these chores as spare-time tasks.

After a severe attack of reality, I realized I was spending about 80 percent of my time managing and marketing my business, and 20 percent in creative pursuits. Meanwhile, though, I was also establishing a marketable reputation that would eventually enable me to improve that ratio.

No matter what sort of photographic service you're engaged in, your most important product is professionalism. You must establish a reputation for reliability, competence, punctuality, courtesy, superior services, sacred deadlines, and guaranteed satisfaction.

PUBLICITY AND PROMOTION

Publicity is one kind of advertising money can't buy. Advertising is a concentrated and focused effort that you pay for and exercise some control over. Although you can and should guide publicity and control it as best you can, you might not have the final word here; someone else probably will.

Publicity has the same goal as advertising—to get your business known and recognized by potential clients or customers—but is accomplished in different ways. Good publicity is far more valuable than advertising for the very fact that it isn't paid for. Consequently, it seems more like unsolicited endorsement, which it often is.

It's important to get your name before the public at every opportunity. As with advertising, the greatest effects of publicity are cumulative, so it's equally important to keep your name and business image prominent and visible to potential clients.

Organizations

A number of organizations can help you in a variety of ways. National professional and business associations can offer helpful hints and provide a useful exchange of ideas. Association with your peers across the nation can lead to important business contacts.

Local business, fraternal, and other organizations can do much to publicize and promote your business and put you in touch with people you need to know—prospective clients or business associates. I met and got to know both my attorney and my insurance agent when we three worked as committee members for a local chapter of a national conservation organization. I made other significant contacts through the same association. Donating my time and work to the organization also got my business a good bit of publicity.

Some associations worth investigating are your local chamber of commerce, Jaycees, Junior League, Lions Club, Rotary, and Kiwanis. And don't overlook the special-interest clubs and associations.

Media Publicity

A little media publicity can go a long way toward getting your name and business reputation known in your community. What's more, capturing local media attention might be a lot easier than you think.

Newspapers of all sizes run business profiles and features on local entrepreneurs. Small-town and suburban weeklies are the surest bets, but dailies also use such stories.

Visit the newspaper offices in your area, and talk to the appropriate business editor, features editor, managing editor, or whoever else assigns such stories. Keep in mind that it's best to have an angle or peg for the story.

Perhaps you have an interest or specialty that will add appeal to the story about your business. Do you use any unusual techniques or equipment in your photography? Do you shoot scenics with a camera you built yourself? Do you work with old-fashioned or antique cameras? At the other end of the spectrum, maybe you work with the latest high-tech equipment to produce digital imagery or classy multimedia presentations.

Of course, the best peg is the business you're in. Photography is an important part of every newspaper, so take along a portfolio of your best work when you visit an editor. A story about you and your business, illustrated with examples of your work, is invaluable.

Local radio and television stations often air interview and talk shows that can prove good sources of publicity. TV stations also use color stills in horizontal format and can offer opportunities to showcase your work.

PUBLIC RELATIONS

Another way to exploit print and electronic media is with public relations (PR) techniques. For instance, you can use news releases to get the word out about you and your business—but you should have a good news peg to make your release irresistible.

News releases differ from the kind of publicity we discussed earlier in that you furnish the copy to the media. You generate the story, either by writing it yourself or by hiring someone else to write it.

There's nothing wrong with writing your own news releases, providing you possess the necessary skills. If you can't tell a semicolon from a semiconductor, however, get help.

Some editors will use your releases with little or no modification. Others might follow up with phone calls to augment the material you furnish. Still others might assign a reporter and photographer to do a feature or picture spread.

Even if there's nothing particularly unusual or exciting about your business, you can still use public relations to your advantage. Special events, awards, and honors are always good news pegs. So when you win "best of show" at a juried photography exhibition or take three blue ribbons in photography at the county fair, make sure your local print and electronic media know about it. When a professional association elects you to high office or presents you with an award, get out a news release.

News-Release Format

News releases should follow a standard format that includes all pertinent information. You can use plain white paper or your letterhead. You might want to design a news-release form that incorporates your logo.

Make sure your business name, address, and phone number appear prominently at the top of the page. The words *News Release* should also appear in large boldface type near the top of the page. Also include the current date, length, the release date, and the name and phone number of the person to contact for further information.

For releases going to print media, provide the length as an approximate number of words. It's best to keep them brief, usually no more than 200 to 300 words, never more than 500.

Releases for the electronic media should be shorter yet, with length expressed in seconds. You'll have to read them out loud at a normal broadcast pace, and time them. Try to confine them to thirty seconds. You can also provide several versions of the same release running differ-

PHOTO IMAGES UNLIMITED

1492 Columbus Drive ■ Moon Valley, IN 54321 ■ Phone: (123) 555–4545 ■ Fax: (123) 555–6767

NEWS RELEASE

TO: _____ DATE: _____

_____ LENGTH: _____

RELEASE DATE: _____

CONTACT: Kim Watson, Owner/Manager

Title, Headline, or Topic

(more)

ent lengths—say, twenty, thirty, and forty seconds. The recipient can then pick whichever one fits an available time slot.

The release date can be the same as the date you prepared and mailed the release, or some later date, tied to an event. Your release might have a limited life or time span, which you should indicate on the release date line. For example, if the release should run only during the month of July, the release date should be July 1 through July 31.

Below the information lines, immediately preceding the text of the release, center a title, headline, or description of contents.

If a release requires more than one page, all pages except the first should be numbered sequentially and should carry an abbreviated title at the top. At the bottom of every page except the last, enclose the word *more* inside parentheses. At the end of the text, two spaces beneath the final paragraph, center the words *The End* or the symbol # # #.

Use simple sentences and short paragraphs. Avoid jargon and technical language. Use what's known as the inverse-pyramid style, in which you attempt to put all the essential information into the first paragraph or two and the least important material toward the end. That way, an editor can trim it from the end to accommodate space limitations.

Remember the five Ws and the H—Who, What, Where, When, Why, and How—and make sure every release answers each of those.

Showing Your Work

The more people who see your photographs, the greater the cumulative effect and the better the likelihood that potential clients will think of you when they need the services of a competent photographer. So you must take advantage of every opportunity to publicize your photography.

The obvious places to display salon prints are galleries and museums, but there are other places too many photographers overlook. Of course, you should try to sell your work to galleries, and you should enter your photographs in exhibit competition. Talk to gallery owners about handling your work and museum curators about sponsoring one-person shows.

Any business or institution with a lobby, great hall, waiting room, or reception area is a potential client or displayer: banks, clinics, hospitals, dental offices, law offices, executive offices, nursing homes, retirement facilities, senior centers, restaurants, hotels, motels, bed-and-breakfast inns, resorts, charter services, tackle shops, ski shops, dive shops, and the list goes on.

You should be able to sell framed salon prints to these and other establishments. Those who aren't interested in buying often can be persuaded to display a selection of prints in exchange for their decorative value. Others might agree to display and sell your prints on consignment.

In my community, a number of banks display original art and photography as a way of helping artists and photographers to get their work before the public. One retirement complex regularly sponsors and publicizes art and photographic exhibits. Restaurants and resorts up and down the West Coast similarly display the works of local artists and photographers.

Donating Your Work

Making donations to local fund-raisers also can net you some promotional rewards. Depending on the nature of your photography, you might donate a portrait sitting, custom printing, gift certificate, or framed salon print.

When a local nonprofit organization sponsors a fund-raising dinner, auction, or sale, the press is sure to cover the event, and you can share the promotional value when you are listed as one of the donors to the cause.

Volunteering Your Time and Skills

Volunteering is another way to reap the rewards of publicity. You can volunteer to cover events sponsored by local nonprofit organizations. The organizations will be grateful for your help, and local media will be glad to run your photographs with credit lines.

If you can teach what you know about photography, offer to teach a one-day or weekend photography workshop through a local organization or government agency. Such a workshop will call for advance publicity in the form of newspaper articles and public-service announcements on radio and television.

YOUR PORTFOLIO

Many prospective clients will want to see samples of your work before they hire you. You should begin at once to compile a good portfolio—a representative sampling of photographs that demonstrate your skills and versatility.

A portfolio is a growing, expanding collection. In it should be examples of your various specialties: portraits, still lifes, architectural shots, landscapes, wildlife, photojournalism, or whatever else you enjoy shooting.

Don't expect to remember all the negatives and transparencies in your files that are suitable portfolio material. Identify them in some way for easy retrieval. In my photographic filing system, I have negative cards and transparency sheets labeled "Portfolio" with suitable photographs listed and identified there as well as in their respective categories.

Your portfolio will eventually grow far too large to lug to any one showing. So you should carefully choose relevant images to show to any potential client.

Naturally, you should pick your best work for your portfolio. Prints should be as technically perfect as possible, meticulously mounted, and housed in a portfolio box or case. Transparencies should be in flat-black presentation sleeves or mats that can be examined on a light table. Some art directors prefer to project 35mm slides, which you can store and present in Kodak Carousel or Ektagraphic slide trays. Projection can damage your slides, so it's best to submit good-quality duplicates to anyone who wants to project them.

Portfolio boxes and cases are available from various sources in standard sizes ranging from 8 by 10 inches to 24 by 30 inches. The most common sizes for mounted portfolio prints are 11 by 14 inches and 16 by 20 inches.

If you need to send your portfolio to distant clients, use heavy-duty print-shipping cases designed for such purposes.

MOUNTING, MATTING, AND FRAMING PHOTOGRAPHS

Nothing detracts more from the beauty of a good photograph than a bad job of mounting, matting, and framing. Although to do it right, you'll need to learn about the various principles, materials, techniques, and tools, it's not difficult. It requires care and patience, but anyone who can handle a camera can certainly learn to prepare photographs for display.

You can cut mounting boards by using a straightedge and a sharp utility or X-Acto knife. For mounting prints to the boards, you'll find a variety of aerosol mounting adhesives and mounting sheets.

The use of a mat or mats is up to you, but you should know that they are both decorative and functional. The right mat or combination of mats can complement a photograph and provide the perfect professional touch. Mats also help protect framed prints by creating a necessary air space between the print surface and any glass or acrylic used for glazing.

Fine-looking bevel-cut mats appear difficult to make but are actually simple with the right tools. An inexpensive bevel-mat cutter and guide, such as Alto's E-Z Mat System, will have you cutting mats like a pro after only a few minutes' practice.

With a simple miter box and backsaw, you can build your own frames, or you can buy ready-made frames. One kind of frame especially popular with photographers is the metal or acrylic section frame that you can assemble or dismantle with a screwdriver.

Section frames are ideal for use with exhibition prints, because you can easily change their contents to fit your needs.

Everything you need to know about mounting, matting, and framing you'll find in my book, *Home Book of Picture Framing* (Stackpole Books, 1988).

ADVERTISING YOUR BUSINESS

Whether or not you need to advertise depends largely on the kind of photography you engage in. Once you've decided or been advised to advertise, you must determine the best, most cost-effective medium or media.

Should You Hire an Agency?

Advertising is expensive, and advertising agencies are more expensive yet. A good agency can do much for the business ready to use its services but can prove too costly for the new entrepreneur.

A better plan for the start-up home-based photography business is a program that relies primarily on self-promotion, publicity, public relations, and limited advertising. There are media staff people who will work with you, and you can do much of the work yourself. You must determine first what advertising avenues are available in your community or working area and then which ones will serve you best.

Advertising Media

Advertising takes many shapes and shows up in a variety of places, from the covers of matchbooks to the sides of buses. The media that photographers most commonly use include the Yellow Pages, newspapers, magazines, radio, television, brochures, direct mail, and specialty advertising. Costs vary widely, as does effectiveness, and each form has its advantages and disadvantages.

- **YELLOW PAGES.** This is one of the most basic forms of advertising. It can amount to a simple listing or an elaborate display ad. Staff is available to help you with layout.

  Advantages: Directories are widely distributed to everyone who has a phone. People who use the Yellow Pages are in the market for services. Directories are kept on hand for a year.

  Disadvantages: This is a passive medium, meaning people can freely choose what ads to read—or not read. Deadline lead times are long. It's usually not a good idea to include price information.

- **NEWSPAPERS.** The larger the newspaper's circulation, the greater the potential effect of its advertising but also the higher its advertising rates will be. Nevertheless, newspapers remain among the most used media for localized advertising.

  Advantages: Newspapers have a high degree of reader acceptance. Ads are available in a great variety of sizes and can be clipped and saved. They can include as much detail and information as you want or can afford.

  Disadvantages: Newspaper ads are relatively expensive. Newspapers are a passive medium and are short-lived (soon discarded). Poor reproduction, a problem at many small newspapers, can spoil photographs you use with your ads.

- **MAGAZINES.** Under the right circumstances, magazine advertising can be effective for certain photographic businesses. Rates are high, often prohibitive, even in some city and regional magazines.

  Advantages: Reproduction is usually superior to that in other print media. Target marketing is most precise. You can include as much detail as you wish, and ads can be clipped and saved.

  Disadvantages: Magazines have long lead times for deadlines. Like other print media, they are passive and are often so cluttered with ads as to encourage readers to skip them.

- **RADIO.** In some places radio proves to be the best medium for small-business advertising. What's more, radio usually offers competitive rates and ready markets.

  Advantages: Radio provides a good way to target a specific group (for example, commercials for high-school portraits on rock-and-roll stations). Commercials can reach a high percentage of the target group. It's an active medium—commercials are hard to avoid or skip over.

  Disadvantages: Large metropolitan areas are cluttered with many stations, which tends to fragment the audience. Commercials must be short, usually with limited details. The most effective time slots can be prohibitively expensive.

- **TELEVISION.** Generally, television is the most effective advertising medium, but it is also the most expensive. The proliferation of cable companies has made cable advertising more competitive and has put TV advertising within the reach of many small businesses. For some photography businesses, it holds promise.

  Advantages: Cable TV is good for reaching specific market segments. A single TV commercial can reach a large audience. Television is a fairly active medium (but less so with the widespread use of video-cassette recorders and remote control). Television also offers an unlimited range of special effects.

  Disadvantages: High production costs top the list and are in addition to actual commercial time. Audiences have been greatly fragmented by the proliferation of cable channels. The best time slots either are taken by national advertisers or are too expensive for small business.

- **BROCHURES.** For certain kinds of photography, brochures can be an effective form of advertising. Although they're of little or no value to photojournalists, publications photographers, and most portrait photographers, brochures can prove worthwhile for commercial, architectural, and graphic-style photographers.

  Advantages: Brochures provide the greatest amount of space for detailed information. They offer the opportunity to showcase your photographic skills and can function as a portfolio. You can use brochures to reach a targeted direct-mail market.

Disadvantages: Brochures are expensive to produce. They can be time-consuming and expensive to distribute.

- **DIRECT MAIL.** Advertising by mail can cost dearly in money and time, but with the right client list and selective mailing, it can be a valuable marketing tool.

  Advantages: Direct-mail campaigns can reach a broad or concentrated market, depending on your needs and approach. This is also an ideal way to distribute brochures to your target markets and to encourage repeat business.

  Disadvantages: Response rates are often low. Postal rates and printing costs continue to rise to levels that are often prohibitive.

- **SPECIALTY ADVERTISING.** This category includes all the promotional paraphernalia, such as pens, pencils, letter openers, digital clocks, calendars, buttons, caps, and other products bearing a business logo and advertising message. Most of these gimmicks probably have greater goodwill value than advertising worth.

  Advantages: Nobody objects to getting these little freebies. You can target your market, and the advertising value lasts as long as the object.

  Disadvantages: Space for advertising is usually very limited. You must buy a large quantity to keep the per-item cost down. Effective distribution can be costly and time consuming.

Tips on Advertising Effectively

Media staff and your local Small Business Development Center can offer helpful hints for getting the most out of your advertising dollar. Meanwhile, here are a few more tips that should help.

- Make sure all your print ads prominently display your name, address, and phone number.

- When advertising on radio, remember that many of the listeners might be on the road and unable to write down your phone number. Refer them to your Yellow Pages ad instead of giving your phone number.

- The greatest effect of advertising is cumulative. It's better to buy a series of several small ads or commercials than a single large one.

- Radio commercials are most effective when tied into simultaneous print ads.

- Don't make your ads and commercials too busy; keep them concise and uncluttered.

- Saturday is usually a poor day to advertise in newspapers; Sunday is a good day.

- A good way to make newspaper ads last longer is to buy space in a weekend supplement or weekly TV and entertainment guide or section.

- The best times for radio commercials are the morning and evening driving slots, usually from 6:00 to 9:00 A.M. and 3:00 to 7:00 P.M.

The Photographer's Advantage

When it comes to advertising, photographers have a distinct advantage over other entrepreneurs: they can barter with print media and sometimes with the TV folks. As a photographer, you operate in an area that's of value to the media. You might be able to swap your work for advertising.

You can sell photographs to weekly and daily newspapers, magazines of every kind, and even local television stations. These are all good markets. You should also be able to wheel and deal with the same markets, exchanging some of your photographs for advertising credit, but make sure you get more in advertising dollars than you would in cash.

If you regularly sell feature photos to your local daily newspaper for $25 each, try to swap for $50 apiece in advertising credit. If a regional magazine offers you $500 for a cover shot, offer to take $1,000 worth of advertising space instead, if it suits your purpose.

THE BEST OF ALL ADVERTISING

The best advertising is another kind you can't buy. It grows out of your reputation and is spread by people who know your work and freely recommend it. It's often called word-of-mouth advertising, which some people consider narrow in scope, or ineffective. In practice, however, it's a wonderfully compounding dividend that you collect on the principal of your good reputation.

Several years ago a large nursing home in my community hired one of the top photographers in town to shoot black-and-white photographs for a brochure. The client was dissatisfied with the photography and showed the work to a good friend and former student of mine, who promptly recommended me. I was hired at my day rate, and I provided a package that pleased my new client.

The owner of the print shop where the brochure was produced was also impressed by the quality of the work and began recommending me to her clients. I have no way of knowing how much word-of-mouth advertising spread from the initial recommendation, but I realize it has meant a lot of business for me.

About a year after the brochure job, the director of the biggest and newest retirement facility in town, which is affiliated with the nursing home, hired me to shoot photographs to accompany ads in a regional magazine.

Some months later the same director phoned to ask if I might have a color scenic in my stock file showing the view of Coos Bay from the hill where the nursing home and retirement facility stand. She told me she wanted a 16-by-20 enlargement to present to a retiring employee. Not only did I provide the exact image she described, but I also sent a no-charge invoice with it as a way of thanking my client for the repeat business.

It doesn't take long for a few recommendations to grow into a solid reputation that will serve you well in your community and beyond. Only days ago I received a stock order from a client in a foreign country who learned of me as a result of some ordinary and local work.

For a small regional magazine in 1990, I shot the cover photo and an inside spread to accompany an article about coastal Oregon's cranberry harvest. The article was timed to coincide with the annual cranberry festival held in the tiny coastal hamlet of Bandon, Oregon, just down the road from where I live.

The manager of the Bandon Chamber of Commerce liked the spread and later recommended me to a woman who procures stock photography for the Oregon Division of Tourism and now sends me stock requests several times a year. She, in turn, recommended me to the production manager of a multimedia production company in Vancouver, British Columbia, who, it turned out, needed hundreds of images of scenic Oregon.

There's no limit to how far a good reputation and word-of-mouth advertising will take you. Coincidentally, developing foreign markets is now one of my major marketing projects.

DEVELOPING NEW PRODUCTS, SERVICES, AND MARKETS

Your business will probably eventually grow to a point of saturation, either yours or the market's. When that happens, you may or may not wish to keep expanding. If you're comfortable with the size of your business and income, your marketing effort can then be reduced to maintaining the status quo and replacing markets that fall by the wayside. By then your reputation might even be such that your business won't need much publicity, promotion, or advertising.

During your business's formative years, or possibly even for the life of your business, you'll need to be concerned with continued growth and increased profits. If you are managing wisely and getting as much as possible out of every dollar you earn and spend, you will need to turn your attention to developing new products, services, and markets as ways of increasing income and profits.

I've been running my own business for more than twenty years, and I still remain alert for new marketing opportunities. I keep a list of markets I haven't yet cracked but would like to. I then try to develop one or several new markets or upgrade existing ones each year.

Identify Your Opportunities

No matter what kinds of photography you do, you'll discover other products and services you can provide and a great number and variety of potential new markets. Before you venture into new areas, though, you need to carefully consider the kinds of work that interest you, the kinds that don't, and those that are of marginal interest. You need to identify and analyze the markets as well. It's equally important to know and understand your limitations.

I enjoy most photographic work, but there's some that doesn't interest me and some for which I just don't have the technical expertise. For example, I've done some portraits, but I don't particularly enjoy portraiture, so I don't pursue it. I would like to produce high-tech commercial photography, and I think I would enjoy multimedia production and digital imagery, but the lack of equipment and expertise keeps me from seriously venturing into these areas.

I try to develop several new markets or categories of markets each year. This year, in addition to investigating the prospects outside U.S. borders, I hope to sell work to several specific magazines I've never worked for and to begin selling work to the category of publications known as "inflights"—the general-interest give-away magazines you find on commercial passenger aircraft.

Many of the publications that now buy my work were once no more than undeveloped target markets on my list of projects for the coming or current year.

I also keep lists of photographic subjects and categories I want to begin working on and those I need to expand to broaden my market base. Such lists can be as general or specific as you want them to be. What's important is that you keep them as reminders of what you need to work on and when.

This year I have given myself the broad and vague command to "build stock." That means I want to make a concerted effort to shoot a lot of stock photos this year, to build up my stock files and to submit to stock agencies.

On a more specific level, I intend to work on one category that has been on my list for years but is sadly lacking. A years-long period of drought seems to have come to an end in Oregon and California. We've had plenty of rain on the coast and snow in the mountains. So this spring, as soon as the foliage has formed and wildflowers have popped up, I'm going waterfall hunting. Coastal mountain streams should be high and obliging. I know I have sufficient equipment and expertise to significantly build my file of waterfall photographs, and by summer I will be marketing images of cascading creeks and silvery sylvan waterfalls I've been waiting to shoot for more than six years.

Even more specific yet is my notation, "Skunk Cabbage." I already have a fair file of pictures of skunk cabbages, interesting plants that are related to the calla lily that grow in some profusion in coastal lowlands. Several summers ago, I found a huge, sprawling patch of the plants with leaves as broad as 3 feet. But the photograph I want must be shot in the late winter or early spring, when the plant's cheery spathes unfold and paint the verdant valley with 10,000 broad brush strokes of bright yellow. That's also the shot that will complete a picture-story I'll sell to a magazine. If I have a good day, I will also collect stock shots and other images that will sell to calendar and postcard markets.

Government Work

Don't overlook the possibility of working for various government agencies that regularly buy work from freelancers or independent contractors. Potential markets exist at all levels of government: city, county, state, and federal.

City and county park and recreation departments are good prospects, as are port authorities and any agencies engaged in promoting tourism.

On the state level are colleges and universities, which publish brochures, catalogs, and other photo-illustrated materials. State departments and divisions that frequently use photographs include fish and wildlife, forestry, ecology, tourism, parks, transportation, agriculture, and economic development.

The sprawling federal government has many departments, bureaus, and services with headquarter offices in Washington, D.C., and with field offices in all the states and many cities, large and small. Some of the most widely represented agencies include the U.S. Fish and Wildlife Service, National Park Service, and U.S. Forest Service.

Even in the small community where I live, we have large Bureau of Land Management and U.S. Coast Guard facilities, as well as offices of the U.S. Army Corps of Engineers, the National Marine Fisheries Service, and the Sanctuaries and Reserves Division of the National Oceanic and Atmospheric Administration, for which I recently worked for six months as an independent contractor.

The Show Must Go On—and On and On and On

At times, I have saturated various markets, especially some of the smaller ones. For example, I have sold so much material to a particular publication or category of publications that I've had to back off for several months to a year to let them use up my material in their inventory.

During tight financial times, some markets just go out of business, which can leave you high and dry if they represent a substantial part of

TWENTY WAYS TO EXPAND
YOUR PHOTOGRAPHY BUSINESS

1. *Model portfolios.* Models need photographs of themselves to present to agencies and potential clients. You can charge as you would for portraits or location shoots, or, if you need models in your work, you can trade your photographic services for model services.

2. *Actor portfolios.* Actors, dancers, and other theatrical artists also need photographs of themselves. Look for prospective clients at local production companies and college or university dramatics departments.

3. *Artist portfolios.* Artists in all media need to keep photographic documentation of their works; often they don't have or don't take the time to do so. Sell your services to them and you will likely get a good bit of return business.

4. *Limited-edition fine-art prints.* Select from your files photographs that lend themselves to enlargement and display. Then create a series of superbly mounted, matted, and framed prints in limited numbers. Then sell them as signed and numbered limited editions.

5. *Advertising photographs of locally made products.* Make yourself aware of all locally made products and remain alert for the introduction of new products. Let the manufacturers know that you are available to shoot advertising and catalog photographs.

6. *Mug shots.* Shoot people and pet portraits and print them on coffee mugs, plates, buttons, and other products sold for such purposes.

7. *Multimedia productions for local companies.* Here's a mighty lucrative endeavor for any photographer or team of collaborators capable of producing presentations that include transparencies, video, music, and narration.

8. *Car-club photographs.* All sorts of clubs exist for collectors of antique and classic cars and trucks, street rods, and customized cars. Attend their shows, and look for good stock-photo opportunities. Distribute business cards and handouts that describe your work and you will probably line up some new clients.

9. *Aircraft and aviator photographs.* Like the auto buffs, hobby aviators spend a lot of money on their pet projects. Attend air shows, hand out promotional material and business cards, get to know the pilots, and offer your services.

10. *Skydiving-club photographs.* Check at local airports for skydiving clubs. Introduce yourself, and offer to provide photographs. Jump if you want, but you don't have to. You can get some outstanding and salable shots from the plane or from the ground.

11. *Hang-glider photographs.* Hang around areas where hang-gliding enthusiasts gather and you will not only gather colorful photographs for your files and for stock sales but probably sell shots to the soarers as well.

12. *Surfing and sailboarding photographs.* If you live along the coast or near lakes and rivers frequented by sailboarders, you'll find good opportunities for colorful action photography that will sell to a variety of markets, including the surfers and sailboarders themselves.

13. *Dental and medical photography.* Many dentists and physicians use photography in their practices. Some undoubtedly would prefer to turn such work over to professional photographers. Research the Yellow Pages, and contact prospective new clients.

14. *Photographs of athletes in action.* Action shots of athletes of all ages and levels are always in demand as publication and stock photography. You can also sell these photos to the athletes. So cover sports events in your area, and take plenty of model releases with you.

15. *Racing photographs.* Races of all sorts—auto, boat, motorcycle, dogsled—are sure bets for good action photography that will sell to local and national media, stock agencies, and the racers themselves.

16. *Bulk film.* You can save money by buying an inexpensive film loader, cassettes, and bulk film, then loading your own. You can make money selling rolls of loaded bulk film to other local photographers. Contact camera clubs, newspapers, and photography departments at high schools and colleges.

17. *Photography and darkroom products.* You don't have to own a store to become a photographic-products dealer. You can sell directly to the same customers who buy your loaded bulk film. Contact manufacturers of cameras, lenses, accessories, and supplies you would like to carry, and ask for their catalogs and dealer's price lists.

18. *Used-car photographs.* Car dealers, large and small, advertise their used cars and trucks. Many use black-and-white photographs with their ads. Deliver business cards and promo sheets to all your local car dealers, and set up a regular weekly route.

19. *Watercraft photographs.* Boat dealers and yacht brokers often use photographs with their newspaper and magazine ads. As with car dealers, try to set up accounts and establish regular routes, or phone once a week to find out if your services are needed.

20. *Framing services.* Custom mounting, matting, and framing represent an aspect of your photography business that can become a lucrative sideline. Learn the craft, and advertise your services.

your income, especially if you don't have alternative markets to fall back on. In 1991 I was not prepared for three of my magazine markets to fold in May and June, at the peak of my most productive time of the year. While I hustled to develop other markets to fill the void and regain my momentum, I lost a good bit of valuable time and income.

I have learned from such experiences that I must continually strive to develop new markets and improve existing ones, but too often I have so much work that I don't have time for that crucial part of my operation. All I can do then is promise myself I will do better when the pressure is off.

Toward that end, I make only one New Year's resolution and repeat it every January 1. I have it printed in bold black on an index card pinned to the bulletin board above my desk. It says simply: WORK SMARTER THIS YEAR!

SELECTED BIBLIOGRAPHY

Attard, Janet. *The Home Office and Small Business Answer Book*. New York: Henry Holt and Company, Inc., 1993.

Blum, Laurie. *Free Money For Small Businesses and Entrepreneurs,* Third Edition. New York: John Wiley & Sons, Inc., 1992.

Dible, Donald, editor. *What Everybody Should Know about Patents, Trademarks and Copyrights*. Prentice Hall, 1982.

Downing, Douglas and Michael Covington. *Dictionary of Computer Terms,* Third Edition. Hauppauge, NY: Barron's, 1992.

The Editors of *Entrepreneur*. *Entrepreneur Magazine's Complete Guide to Owning a Home-Based Business*. New York: Bantam Books, 1990.

Foster, Frank H. and Robert L. Shook. *Patents, Copyrights, and Trademarks,* Second Edition. New York: John Wiley & Sons, 1993.

Godin, Seth, editor. *The Information Please Business Almanac & Desk Reference*. New York: Houghton Mifflin. Published annually.

Gookin, Dan. *DOS for Dummies*. San Mateo, CA: IDG Books Worldwide, Inc., 1991.

———. *WordPerfect 6 for Dummies*. San Mateo, CA: IDG Books Worldwide, Inc., 1993.

Gumpert, David E. *How to Really Start Your Own Business*. Boston: *Inc.* Publishing, 1991.

H&R Block, Inc. *H&R Block Income Tax Guide*. New York: Collier Books. Published annually.

Harper, Stephen C. *Starting Your Own Business: A Step-by-Step Blueprint for the First-Time Entrepreneur*. New York: McGraw-Hill, 1991.

Hart, Russell. *Photographing Your Artwork*. Cincinnati: North Light Books, 1987.

Hedgecoe, John. *The Photographer's Handbook*, Third Edition. New York: Alfred A. Knopf, 1992.

Herring, Jerry and Mark Fulton. *The Art & Business of Creative Self-Promotion*. New York: Watson-Guptill Publications, 1987.

Jacobs, Lou, Jr. *Selling Photographs: Determining Your Rates and Understanding Your Rights*. New York: Amphoto, 1988.

———. *Selling Stock Photography: How to Market Your Photographs for Maximum Profit*. New York: Amphoto, 1992.

J. K. Lasser Institute. *J. K. Lasser's Your Income Tax Guide*. New York: Prentice Hall. Published annually.

Krol, Ed. *The Whole Internet User's Guide and Catalog*. Sebastapol, CA: O'Reilly & Associates, Inc., 1992.

La Quey, Tracy with Jeanne C. Ryer. *The Internet Companion*. Reading, MA: Addison-Wesley Publishing Co., 1993.

Mincberg, Mella. *WordPerfect 6 Made Easy*. Berkeley: Osborne/McGraw-Hill, 1993.

Murphy, John and Michael Rowe. *How to Design Trademarks and Logos*. Cincinnati: North Light Books, 1988.

Muse, Kenneth. *Photo One*, Second Edition. Englewood Cliffs, NJ: Prentice Hall, 1987.

Nunes, Morris A. *Basic Legal Forms for Business*. New York: John Wiley & Sons, Inc., 1993.

O'Hara, Patrick D. *How to Computerize Your Small Business*. New York: John Wiley & Sons, Inc., 1993.

Rue, Leonard Lee III. *How I Photograph Wildlife and Nature*. New York: W. W. Norton & Company, 1984.

Schaub, George. *Shooting for Stock*. New York: Amphoto, 1987.

Stevens, Al. *Teach Yourself Windows 95*. New York: MIS Press, 1995.

Thomas, Bill. *How You Can Make $50,000 a Year as a Nature Photojournalist*. Cincinnati: Writer's Digest Books, 1986.

Tresidder, Jack, editor-in-chief. *Kodak Library of Creative Photography*. 18 volumes. New York: Time-Life Books, 1983–1985.

Willins, Michael, editor. *Photographer's Market*. Cincinnati: Writer's Digest Books. Published annually.

SOURCE DIRECTORY

ASSOCIATIONS

Advertising Photographers of
America
45 East 20th Street
New York, NY 10003
(212) 254-5500

The American Society of Media
Photographers
205 Lexington Avenue
New York, NY 10016
(212) 889-9144

Professional Photographers of
America, Inc.
350 North Wolf Road
Mount Prospect, IL 60056
(800) 742-7468

BUSINESS EQUIPMENT AND SUPPLIES

Fidelity Products Company
5601 International Parkway
P.O. Box 155
Minneapolis, MN 55440
Customer Service: (800) 554-3013
Orders: (800) 328-3034
Fax: (800) 842-2725

Office and graphic-arts equipment and supplies.

NEBS, Inc.
500 Main
Groton, MA 01471
(800) 225-6380
Fax: (800) 234-4324

Business forms, letterhead,
envelopes, business cards, labels,
rubber stamps, and forms software.

Quill Corporation (Rockies and
  East)
P.O. Box 4700
Lincolnshire, IL 60197
Customer Service: (708) 634–8000
Orders: (708) 634–4800
Fax: (708) 634–5708

Quill Corporation (West of
  Rockies)
P.O. Box 50-050
Ontario, CA 91761
Customer Service: (714) 998–3200
Orders: (714) 998–3200
Fax: (708) 634–5708

Full line of business and office
equipment, furniture, fixtures,
and supplies, including computer
hardware and software.

Reliable Home Office
P.O. Box 804117
Chicago, IL 60680
Customer Service: (800) 326–6230
Orders: (800) 869–6000
Fax: (800) 326–3233

Office furniture and fixtures.

Viking Office Products
24 Thompson Road
East Windsor, CT 06088
(800) 421–1222

Full line of office and stationery
supplies, forms, and more, with
facilities in six U.S. regions.

COMPUTER SOFTWARE AND SERVICES

CompuServe
P.O. Box 20212
Columbus, OH 43220
(800) 368–3343 Ext. 35

Computer-information network.

Cradoc CaptionWriter
6962 East First Avenue
Suite 103
Scottsdale, AZ 85251
(602) 945–2001
Fax: (602) 945–1023

Slide-labeling and captioning
software system for Macintosh
and IBM-compatible computers.

Frederick Zimmerman &
  Associates
P.O. Box 1919
Decatur, GA 30031
(404) 633–0179

IBM-compatible slide-labeling
software systems.

General Electric Information
  Services
888 South Figueroa Street, #700
Los Angeles, CA 90017
(213) 236–0200

Computer-information network.

Multiplex Display Fixture
   Company
1555 Larkin Williams Road
Fenton, MO 63026
(800) 325–3350
Fax: (314) 326–1716

Slidebase-Pro image-management
software for IBM-compatible
computers.

Parhelion
P.O. Box 107
Cornish Flat, NH 03746
(603) 675–2966

Macintosh-based Full Spectrum
software for image filing and
management.

Phototrack Software
6392 South Yellowstone Way
Aurora, CO 80016
(303) 690–6664
Fax: (303) 693–4750

Stock-management software for
   IBM-compatible and
   Macintosh computers.

Power Up! Software Corporation
P.O. Box 7600
San Mateo, CA 94403
(800) 851–2917
Fax: (415) 345–5575

Business and financial software.

Public Brand Software
P.O. Box 51315
Indianapolis, IN 46251
(800) 426–3475
Fax: (317) 856–2086

Business and financial software
and shareware.

Reasonable Solutions
1221 Disk Drive
Medford, OR 97501
Information: (503) 776–5777
Orders: (800) 876–3475
Fax: (503) 773–7803

Business and financial software
and shareware.

SlideScribe
7521 Washington Avenue South
Minneapolis, MN 55439
(800) 345–4118
Fax: (612) 942–7852

Image-management software for
Macintosh and IBM-compatible
computers.

COURSES AND SEMINARS

New York Institute of
   Photography
211 East 43rd Street
New York, NY 10017
(800) 336–6947

The Nikon School
1300 Walt Whitman Road
Melville, NY 11747
(516) 547–4200

Winona School of Professional
   Photographers
350 North Wolf Road
Mount Prospect, IL 60056
(800) 742–7468

MAGAZINES

Entrepreneur Magazine and
   Business Guides
2392 Morse Avenue
Irvine, CA 92714
(714) 261–2325
California: (800) 352–7449
Elsewhere: (800) 421–2300

Inc. Publishing
38 Commercial Wharf
Boston, MA 02110
(617) 227–4700

Industrial Photography
445 Broad Hollow Road
Melville, NY 11747
(516) 845–2700
Fax: (516) 845–7109

Free subscriptions to qualifying
professionals.

Outdoor & Travel Photography
1115 Broadway, Eighth Floor
New York, NY 10010
(212) 807–7100
Fax: (212) 229–1897

Outdoor Photographer
Werner Publishing Corporation
12121 Wilshire Boulevard
Suite 1220
Los Angeles, CA 90025
(310) 820–1500

Popular Photography (editorial
   offices)
1633 Broadway
New York, NY 10019
(212) 767–6000

Popular Photography (subscription
   offices)
P.O. Box 54912
Boulder, CO 80322

Photo Electronic Imaging
1090 Executive Way
Des Plaines, IL 60018
(708) 299–8161
Fax: (708) 299–2685

Free subscription to qualifying
professionals.

PHOTOGRAPHIC EQUIPMENT AND SUPPLIES

Alto's EZ/Mat, Inc.
607 West Third Avenue
Ellensburg, WA 98926
(509) 962–9212

Mat cutters and mat-cutting systems.

The BD Company
P.O. Box 1591
New York, NY 10156
(800) 704–3072

Seamless backgrounds and stands.

Calumet Photographic, Inc.
890 Supreme Drive
Bensenville, IL 60106
(708) 860–7447 Ext. 231
(800) 225–8638
Fax: (708) 860–5168

Publishes a big catalog full of 35mm, medium-format, and large-format cameras, lenses, and accessories; studio and darkroom equipment and supplies; and much more.

Canon U.S.A., Inc.
1 Canon Plaza
Lake Success, NY 11042
(516) 328–4828

Full line of 35mm cameras, lenses, and accessories.

The Denny Manufacturing
Company, Inc.
P.O. Box 7200
Mobile, AL 36670
(205) 457–2388
Orders: (800) 888–5616
Fax: (205) 452–4630

Photographic backgrounds, stands, and props.

Eastman Kodak Company
343 State Street
Rochester, NY 14650
(716) 724–2364

Films, papers, chemicals, projection equipment, and much more. Many technical publications available.

Freestyle
5124 Sunset Boulevard
Los Angeles, CA 90027
(213) 660–3460

Photographic equipment and supplies.

Fuji Photo Film, U.S.A., Inc.
555 Taxter Road
Elmsford, NY 10523
(914) 789–8100
Fax: (914) 682–4955 or 682–4956

Major film manufacturer.

Graphic Dimensions, Ltd.
41–23 Haight Street
Flushing, NY 11355
(718) 463-3500
Orders: (800) 221-0262
Fax: (718) 463-2470

Large selection of custom-made
and ready-made picture frames,
including section frames.

Light Impressions
439 Monroe Avenue
Rochester, NY 14603
(716) 271-8960

Full line of archival mounting,
matting, storage, mailing, and
transport supplies.

Mamiya America Corporation
8 Westchester Plaza
Elmsford, NY 10523
(914) 347-3300
Fax: (914) 347-3309

Medium-format and 35mm cameras, lenses, and accessories.

Minolta Corporation
100 Williams Drive
Ramsey, NJ 07446
(201) 825-4000 Ext. 5217
Fax: (201) 818-3590

Full line of 35mm cameras, lenses,
and accessories.

Nikon, Inc.
1300 Walt Whitman Road
Melville, NY 11747
(516) 547-4200

Enlarger lenses and full line of
35mm cameras, lenses, and accessories.

Norman Camera and Video
3602 South Westnedge
Kalamazoo, MI 49008
(616) 345-0164
Fax: (616) 343-6410

Full line of brand-name equipment and supplies.

Olympus America, Inc.
Consumer Products Group
145 Crossways Park West
Woodbury, NY 11797
(516) 364-3000
Fax: (516) 677-1699

Full line of 35mm cameras, lenses,
and accessories.

Pentax Corporation
35 Inverness Drive East
Englewood, CO 80155
(800) 877-0155
Fax: (303) 799-9213

Medium-format and 35mm cameras, lenses, and accessories.

Print File, Inc.
P.O. Box 607638
Orlando, FL 32860
(407) 886-3100
Fax: (407) 886-0008

Archivally safe negative and transparency filing pages and systems.

Tiffen Manufacturing
   Corporation
90 Oser Avenue
Hauppauge, NY 11788
(516) 273-2500
Fax: (516) 273-2557

A large line of photographic filters and lens attachments.

Vue-All, Inc.
P.O. Drawer 1690
Ocala, FL 34478
(904) 732-3188
Fax: (904) 867-8243

Archivally safe negative and transparency filing pages.

Yashica/Contax
100 Randolph Road
Somerset, NJ 08875
(800) 526-0266

Full line of cameras, lenses, and accessories.

U.S. GOVERNMENT

Internal Revenue Service
Eastern Area Distribution Center
P.O. Box 85074
Richmond, VA 23261

Central Area Distribution Center
P.O. Box 8903
Bloomington, IL 61702

Western Area Distribution Center
Rancho Cordova, CA 95743

Small Business Administration
   (SBA)
1441 L Street Northwest
Washington, DC 20416
(202) 653-6600

SBA Publications
P.O. Box 30
Denver, CO 80201

Superintendent of Documents
U.S. Government Printing Office
Washington, DC 20402

U.S. Copyright Office
Library of Congress Building
Department D5
Washington, DC 20402
(202) 783-3238

U.S. Patent Office
2021 Jefferson Davis Highway
Arlington, VA 20231
(703) 557-3158

_____ **/** _____

Appointments/Meetings:

1. _____
2. _____
3. _____
4. _____
5. _____

Must Do (Priority 1):

1. _____
2. _____
3. _____
4. _____
5. _____
6. _____
7. _____
8. _____
9. _____
10. _____

Should Do (Priority 2):

1. _____
2. _____
3. _____
4. _____
5. _____
6. _____
7. _____
8. _____
9. _____
10. _____

Try To Do (Priority 3):

1. _____
2. _____
3. _____
4. _____
5. _____
6. _____
7. _____
8. _____

Phone/E-mail/Letters:

1. _____
2. _____
3. _____
4. _____
5. _____
6. _____
7. _____
8. _____
9. _____
10. _____

Notes/Reminders:

_____
_____
_____
_____
_____
_____
_____
_____
_____
_____
_____

Journal:

_____
_____
_____
_____
_____
_____
_____
_____
_____
_____
_____
_____
_____

_____ / _____   _____ / _____

Notes: _____   Notes: _____
_____   _____
_____   _____
_____   _____
_____   _____

Appointments/Meetings: Appointments/Meetings:
_____   _____
_____   _____
_____   _____
_____   _____

Phone/E-mail/Correspondence: Phone/E-mail/Correspondence:
_____   _____
_____   _____
_____   _____
_____   _____
_____   _____
_____   _____
_____   _____
_____   _____

Must Do Today (Priority 1):   Must Do Today (Priority 1):
_____   _____
_____   _____
_____   _____
_____   _____
_____   _____
_____   _____
_____   _____
_____   _____

Should Do Today (Priority 2):   Should Do Today (Priority 2):
_____   _____
_____   _____
_____   _____

_____ / _____   **JOURNAL**

Notes: _____

_____

_____

_____

_____

Appointments/Meetings:

_____

_____

_____

_____

Phone/E-mail/Correspondence:

_____

_____

_____

_____

_____

_____

Must Do Today (Priority 1):   Next Week:

_____

_____

_____

_____

_____

_____

Should Do Today (Priority 2):

_____

_____

_____

MONDAY: _____ / _____

Notes: _____
_____
_____
_____
_____

To Do Today:

1. _____
2. _____
3. _____
4. _____
5. _____
6. _____
7. _____
8. _____
9. _____
10. _____
11. _____
12. _____

TUESDAY: _____ / _____

Notes: _____
_____
_____
_____
_____

To Do Today:

1. _____
2. _____
3. _____
4. _____
5. _____
6. _____
7. _____
8. _____
9. _____
10. _____
11. _____
12. _____

WEDNESDAY: _____ / _____

Notes: _____
_____
_____
_____
_____

To Do Today:

1. _____
2. _____
3. _____
4. _____
5. _____
6. _____
7. _____
8. _____
9. _____
10. _____
11. _____
12. _____

THURSDAY: _____ / _____

Notes: _____
_____
_____
_____
_____

To Do Today:

1. _____
2. _____
3. _____
4. _____
5. _____
6. _____
7. _____
8. _____
9. _____
10. _____
11. _____
12. _____

FRIDAY: _____ / _____

Notes: _____
_____
_____
_____
_____

To Do Today:
1. _____
2. _____
3. _____
4. _____
5. _____
6. _____
7. _____
8. _____
9. _____
10. _____
11. _____
12. _____

SATURDAY: _____ / _____

Notes: _____
_____
_____
_____
_____

To Do Today:
1. _____
2. _____
3. _____
4. _____
5. _____
6. _____
7. _____
8. _____
9. _____
10. _____
11. _____
12. _____

SUNDAY: _____ / _____

Notes: _____
_____
_____
_____
_____

To Do Today:
1. _____
2. _____
3. _____
4. _____
5. _____
6. _____
7. _____
8. _____
9. _____
10. _____
11. _____
12. _____

JOURNAL

_____
_____
_____
_____
_____
_____
_____
_____
_____
_____
_____

Next Week:

_____
_____
_____
_____
_____
_____
_____

WEEK: _____ / _____

Appointments/Meetings:

_____

_____

_____

_____

_____

_____

Notes/Reminders:

_____

_____

_____

_____

_____

_____

Photography:

1. _____
2. _____
3. _____
4. _____
5. _____
6. _____
7. _____
8. _____
9. _____
10. _____
11. _____
12. _____
13. _____
14. _____
15. _____
16. _____
17. _____
18. _____
19. _____
20. _____

Phone/E-mail/Letters:

1. _____
2. _____
3. _____
4. _____
5. _____
6. _____
7. _____
8. _____
9. _____
10. _____
11. _____
12. _____
13. _____
14. _____
15. _____

Chores:

1. _____
2. _____
3. _____
4. _____
5. _____
6. _____
7. _____
8. _____
9. _____
10. _____
11. _____
12. _____
13. _____
14. _____
15. _____

Top Prority/Must Do:

1. _____
2. _____
3. _____
4. _____
5. _____
6. _____
7. _____
8. _____
9. _____
10. _____

Appointments/Meetings:

_____
_____
_____
_____
_____
_____
_____
_____

Top Priority/Must Do:

_____
_____
_____
_____
_____
_____
_____
_____

Photography:

_____
_____
_____
_____
_____
_____
_____
_____
_____
_____
_____
_____
_____
_____
_____
_____
_____
_____
_____
_____
_____

Business/Household Chores:

_____
_____
_____
_____
_____
_____
_____
_____
_____
_____
_____
_____
_____
_____
_____
_____
_____
_____
_____
_____
_____

QUARTER _____

January Projects:

_____
_____
_____
_____
_____
_____
_____
_____
_____
_____
_____
_____
_____
_____

February Projects:

_____
_____
_____
_____
_____
_____
_____
_____
_____
_____
_____
_____
_____

March Projects:

_____
_____
_____
_____
_____
_____
_____
_____
_____
_____
_____
_____
_____
_____

Household Projects:

_____
_____
_____
_____
_____
_____
_____
_____
_____
_____
_____
_____
_____

Deadlines:

_____
_____
_____
_____
_____
_____
_____
_____
_____
_____

Royalties Due:

_____
_____
_____
_____
_____
_____
_____
_____
_____
_____

INDEX